The Book of Five Rings

by Miyamoto Musashi

Level 5

Translated by Nishiumi Coen
and Michael Brase

IBC パブリッシング

はじめに

　ラダーシリーズは、「はしご（ladder）」を使って一歩一歩上を目指すように、学習者の実力に合わせ、無理なくステップアップできるよう開発された英文リーダーのシリーズです。

　リーディング力をつけるためには、繰り返したくさん読むこと、いわゆる「多読」がもっとも効果的な学習法であると言われています。多読では、「1. 速く　2. 訳さず英語のまま　3. なるべく辞書を使わず」に読むことが大切です。スピードを計るなど、速く読むよう心がけましょう（たとえば TOEIC® テストの音声スピードはおよそ 1 分間に150 語です）。そして 1 語ずつ訳すのではなく、英語を英語のまま理解するくせをつけるようにします。こうして読み続けるうちに語感がついてきて、だんだんと英語が理解できるようになるのです。まずは、ラダーシリーズの中からあなたのレベルに合った本を選び、少しずつ英文に慣れ親しんでください。たくさんの本を手にとるうちに、英文書がすらすら読めるようになってくるはずです。

《本シリーズの特徴》

- 中学校レベルから中級者レベルまで5段階に分かれています。自分に合ったレベルからスタートしてください。
- クラシックから現代文学、ノンフィクション、ビジネスと幅広いジャンルを扱っています。あなたの興味に合わせてタイトルを選べます。
- 巻末のワードリストで、いつでもどこでも単語の意味を確認できます。レベル1、2では、文中の全ての単語が、レベル3以上は中学校レベル外の単語が掲載されています。
- カバーにヘッドホーンマークのついているタイトルは、オーディオ・サポートがあります。ウェブから購入／ダウンロードし、リスニング教材としても併用できます。

《使用語彙について》

レベル1：中学校で学習する単語約1000語

レベル2：レベル1の単語＋使用頻度の高い単語約300語

レベル3：レベル1の単語＋使用頻度の高い単語約600語

レベル4：レベル1の単語＋使用頻度の高い単語約1000語

レベル5：語彙制限なし

Contents

The Book of Earth 1

The Book of Water 27

The Book of Fire 59

The Book of Wind 89

The Book of Emptiness 109

Word List 114

The Book of Earth

The Book of Earth　地の巻

　宮本武蔵が自らの流派「二天一流」を名乗り、これまでの
生涯と兵法の概要を述べた巻。文武両道の重要性や、武器
の使い分け、兵法の拍子や掟などを説く。大工に例えて兵
法の極意を説明する。

【主な難しい用語や表現】

ページ

3	martial arts	武芸
4	art of strategy	兵法
	proficiency	熟達
5	tread	足を踏み入れる
6	inner meaning	奥義
8	discernment	優れた判断力
	perpetuation	永続化
	social standing	家格
	deftness	器用さ, 熟練さ
10	scaffolding	足場
	decorative alcove	床の間
	grooved beam	鴨居
11	adze	手おの
	tabernacle	厨子《仏具》
13	get flustered	動揺する
16	halberd	長刀
	at close quarters	間近に, 接近して
18	musket	鉄砲
20	encirclement	包囲
21	quirk	癖
	foot soldier	足軽
22	come down in the world	落ちぶれる

Thinking that I would put down in writing for the first time what I have learned over the years about military strategy and tactics, which I call *Ni Ten Ichi Ryū*, I climbed Mt. Iwato in Higo in the 10th month of the 20th year of the Kan'ei era [1643] to pray to Heaven, pay my respects to Kannon, and present myself before the Buddha. I am a samurai hailing from Harima. My age is 60, and my name is Shinmen Musashi no Kami, Fujiwara no Genshin.

I have studied martial arts from my youth, and had my first duel at the age of 13. My opponent was a martial artist named Arima Kihei of the Shintō school. When 16 I defeated a formidable swordsman from Tajima named Akiyama. When 21 I went to Kyoto and challenged well-known martial artists there numerous times and was never defeated. Thereafter I roamed the country, meeting martial artists of various sorts, and fought more than 60 times, but never once did I lose. This all took place from the time I was 13 until I was 28 or 29.

Looking back on the days when I was just past

30, I cannot say, even then, that I had yet mastered the art of strategy. It may be that I was able to gain proficiency in the Way of the martial arts because I was born to it, or it may be that the other schools were not really that good.

Finally, after training day and night to uncover the secrets of the Way of the warrior, I reached the age of 50 before attaining mastery.

Since then, without new paths to explore, I spend the passing days as they come and go. Further, following what I have learned from the martial arts, I am trying to master other arts, in all of which I have no teacher. Even now, as I prepare to put my thoughts on paper, I am not relying on the teachings of Buddhism or Confucianism; neither do I refer to old war chronicles or military tactics. But simply adhering to the Way of *Ni Ten Ichi Ryū*, I took up my brush and began writing at daybreak on the 10th day of the 10th month in order to reveal the truth of the Way and the Way of Heaven, as well as the truth revealed by Kannon.

Strategy embodies the rules of samurai life. Leaders especially should put these rules into practice, and lower-ranking samurai should be familiar with them. In the world today there is not a single samurai who really knows the rules of strategy.

While many people follow the path of Buddhism for its merciful kindness, Confucianism for its learning, and medicine for its healing powers, not to mention poetry, tea ceremony, archery, and various other pursuits to which people devote themselves, you rarely find anyone pursuing the Way of strategy.

What a samurai should do first is to cultivate both the literary and martial arts, both the pen and the sword. Even if you should lack talent and are found wanting, you should nonetheless pursue these two paths as best you can.

Most fundamental of all is that samurai should meet death in the most admirable way possible. When it comes to dying, not only samurai but also Buddhist priests, women, and peasants should consider when they are to die, whether it be from a sense of duty or a sense of shame.

Above all else, for a samurai to tread the Way of strategy means to be superior to others in every way. From one-on-one encounters to large-scale engagements, the goal is to emerge victorious, make a name for yourself and rise in the world, both for the sake of your lord and for yourself. This is the virtue of the Way of strategy.

Among those who have studied strategy, there are some who are useless in actual battle. In that regard, we can only say that the real road of military strategy is to instruct students to be effective in every sort of situation, to practice toward that end, and always be useful in actual combat.

The Way of Strategy

Both in China and in Japan, those who have traveled this path are known as masters of the Way of strategy. For a samurai, it is absolutely essential to study this art. These days, however, there are those who pass themselves off as masters of strategy but who, in fact, are only good with a sword.

In a recent happening, the priests of Kashima Katori shrine in Hitachi set up a martial arts school, saying it was passed down from the deity they worship, and sent its members around the country in search of new adherents.

From olden times, people thought that some of the so-called Ten Talents and Seven Arts could be used to make a profit. While this was not said solely in reference to sword fighting, those who seek superficial profit from the sword will not penetrate its inner meaning. Naturally, this also applies to the acquisition of the art of strategy.

Looking around, we see some who sell their various talents almost as if they were selling their body. The same applies to those selling various martial arts equipment; it is like a flower and a seed, when the flower is pretty but the seed is without much meat.

Particularly in the Way of strategy, if you try to make a profit by creating flamboyant displays and boasting that this is the Way of the sword, or establish a *dōjō* to teach and make money from students, you will only be confirming the words that someone spoke: "Half-baked military strategy is the road to great injury."

To make one's way in this world, there are four possible paths.

First is the Way of the peasant. This entails spending one's day loaded down with various tools and keeping an observant eye on the changing seasons and weather.

Second is the Way of commerce. The sake maker has his tools at hand, knows their strengths and weaknesses, and thus makes his way in the world. This is the Way of the merchant, who makes a profit from people's work and thereby sets himself up in life.

Third is the Way of the samurai. The Way of the

samurai consists of the samurai having weapons suitable for every occasion and knowing the strengths and weaknesses of each weapon.

Given the fact that many samurai don't know their weapons, nor how to effectively use them, it can probably be said that present-day samurai are somewhat lacking in discernment.

Fourth is the path of the craftsman or artisan. The carpenter, for example, has a clever mastery of his various tools, knows how to effectively use them, makes his measurements with line and ink, and sets himself up in the world through the continued use of these skills.

These, then, are the four paths through life: that of samurai, peasant, craftsman, and merchant.

The Way of the samurai can be described in terms of the carpenter's path. An analogy with carpentry requires us to think about "houses" or families: for example, noble houses, warrior houses, the four Fujiwara families. The fall of such houses or their perpetuation, their customs, their manner and style, and their social standing—all of these can be looked at from the perspective of carpentry.

In Chinese characters, the word for carpentry means "great deftness," which we would like to consider from the point of view of strategy.

If you want to learn strategy, use this book as a reference, with the teacher being the needle and the student being the thread, and practice tirelessly.

Comparing the Way of the Strategy to Carpentry

The head of a warrior house is the same as a chief carpenter. The head of a house must know the world he governs, rectify the ways of his domain, and keep his house in order, doing the work of a leader of men.

A chief carpenter must know the measurements of halls and temples, and know how to build towers and palaces, employing many people and building many houses. Thus it can be said that the ways of thinking of a chief carpenter and the leader of a warrior house are the same.

For instance, in building a house, the placement of the timber must be considered. For readily visible spaces, straight and handsome wood without knots is selected; for non-visible areas, sturdy straight wood is used, even if it has a few knots. For the threshold, grooved beams, doors and sliding screens, knotless handsome wood is used. Even if the wood has knots or is not straight, as long as it is strong and fits the construction of the house, the house won't become warped or misshapen for a long time. Wood that is knotty, bent, and weak can be used for scaffolding and later for firewood.

When a chief carpenter employs other carpenters beneath him, he must know their strengths and weaknesses, using some of them for the decorative alcove, some for the sliding doors, thresholds, grooved beams, ceilings, and so on, each to what he is best suited. Those with no particular talent can be set to laying floor beams, and those largely untrained to shaving wedges. In this way, by realizing who is fit for what, work can proceed efficiently and smoothly.

Much depends on the chief carpenter's discerning eye: encouraging efficiency and proficiency, providing firm direction, knowing who to use and where, seeing who has spirit and how much, providing encouragement, and knowing everyone's limits.

These same principles apply to strategy as well.

The Way of the Strategist

The ordinary samurai is the same as a carpenter.

A carpenter sharpens his tools himself, having gathered those that are needed, and stores them in a toolbox for safekeeping. When he receives orders from the chief carpenter, he sets to shaping pillars and beams with an adze, smoothing the wood for shelves with a plane, creating wood engravings and openworks, and efficiently completing other delicate tasks after making meticulous measurements. This is what a carpenter does.

If you study these skills and understand the rules of measurement, you can later become a chief carpenter yourself. It is the custom of carpenters to have sharpened tools, and it is important to hone them whenever there is a spare moment. Using those tools the carpenter can cleverly make Buddhist tabernacles, bookshelves, tables, lanterns, and everything from cutting boards to pot lids. This is something only a carpenter can do.

And you should not forget that the same applies to anyone called a samurai. Most important of all, the carpenter habitually takes painstaking care to see that joints fit seamlessly, that the planing is done properly, and that there is no need for later adjustment because the measurements don't match or because the wood has shifted out of place.

Likewise, anyone aspiring to becoming a swordsman should commit to memory each and every item written here.

The Reason This Work Consists of Five Books

I have divided this work into five books in order to bring out the essential nature of the five paths of the strategist: namely, Earth, Water, Fire, Wind, and Emptiness.

In the Book of Earth I will give an outline of military strategy as well as the strategy of my own school.

A true understanding of the Way of strategy cannot be achieved through swordsmanship alone. From the big picture we proceed to the details; from the shallows we proceed to the depths. From the notion of scratching clear guidelines in the soil, I have called this the Book of Earth.

The second book is called the Book of Water. Taking water as our ideal model, we make our hearts like water.

Water fits into a square container as well as a round one, and it can consist of a single drop or it can be an ocean. Water is pure blue, and because of its purity, it lends itself to a discussion of my school.

Here we get a general understanding of the nature of swordsmanship, and learn that if we can defeat one opponent in battle, we can defeat all the people in the world in battle. To defeat one enemy is to defeat a myriad.

For the head of a samurai household, to take a small thing and enlarge it into something big is equivalent to constructing a giant Buddhist statue using a one-foot mold. But I can't go into every detail. From one thing you must understand ten thousand; this is how strategy should be explained. This is the book in which I will discuss my own school.

The third book is the Book of Fire. Here I will discuss fighting. Fire can grow large or be small, and from fire's changeability, it is here that I will discuss battle. The principles of fighting are the same for one-on-one or for 10,000. Taking the big picture or taking the small, you have to always be on the alert.

The big picture is easy to see, the small details are difficult. When attacking in large numbers, sudden tactical change is difficult; when attacking singly, everything can change abruptly depending on the mind of the attacker, so the small things are difficult to predict. Keep this firmly in mind.

This book is about urgent and unexpected situations, and it is essential from a strategic point of view to become accustomed to such situations, to think of them as nothing unusual, and not get flustered. With this in mind, I will discuss large-scale engagements and one-on-one combat in the Book of Fire.

The fourth book is the Book of Wind, which does not take up my own school of strategy. Rather I will describe the various other schools that exist in the world.

"Wind" means the winds of the past, the winds of the present, the gusts of wind created by these various schools, which I will treat in some detail. This is what I mean by "wind."

Without knowing others, you can't know yourself. Even if you follow the Way, even if you train earnestly, there is such a thing as the wrong Way. You may train hard every day and try to achieve perfection, but if you make a slight mistake in approach, even though you still think you are on the right path, it won't look like the true Way to a right-thinking person.

And if you fail to follow the right Way, what is a small mistake in the beginning becomes a big error later on. In regard to other schools, it is thought that sword fighting and only sword fighting is important, and that is probably true for them.

In order to understand the principles and techniques of our school, and their special significance, I will devote the Book of Wind to these other schools.

The fifth book is the Book of Emptiness. There is no front door to the realm of Emptiness and no inner rooms. Just because you have arrived at a certain understanding of the Way does not mean you have to stick persistently to it. The Way of strategy has from the beginning a certain freedom, and as you become more capable, you acquire the right rhythm at the right moment, and in a state of perfect selflessness you attack your enemy and confront your opponent. This is the Way of Emptiness. One day you will naturally acquire an understanding of the true Way. This is the subject of the Book of Emptiness.

Why Our School Is Called *Nitō* (Two Sword)

Samurai, whether commanders or foot soldiers, carry two swords slung from their waists. In the past the long sword was called a *tachi* and the short one a *katana*. Now they are called *katana* and *wakizashi*.

There is no need to give a detailed explanation of why samurai carry two swords. In Japan, regardless of whether you know the reason or not, carrying two swords is the Way of the samurai. *Nitō Ichi Ryū* exists to show the advantages of doing this.

Halberds and spears are called outliers and are used in fights not involving swords.

In my school, the true Way is for beginners to learn by carrying *tachi* and *katana* in both hands. When fighting for one's life, one wants to make use of everything at one's disposal, leaving nothing undone. One doesn't want to be cut down without making use of the full complement of one's weapons.

However, when holding weapons in both hands, it is difficult to freely wield them to the left and right. The *tachi* should be employed with a single hand. The spear and halberd aside, the *katana* and *wakizashi* should be wielded single-handedly.

Employing the *tachi* with both hands proves inconvenient when on horseback, when running, when in a swamp or a rice field, when in rocky terrain, when on a steep incline, or when fighting at close quarters.

And if you are carrying a bow or a spear in your left hand, you have to wield the *tachi* with the single right hand, so it is incorrect to adopt a two-handed stance.

Should it prove impossible to cut down your opponent with a single hand, then it is simply a matter of switching to both hands. Fighting single-handedly is not that difficult. In order to get accustomed to using the *tachi* with one hand, practice flourishing it while holding a sword in the other hand.

At first, anyone will feel the *tachi* to be heavy and difficult to swing. But can't this be said of anything? The bow is hard to draw, the halberd is difficult to wield. As with everything else, it is a matter of getting used to the weapon. In time you gain the strength to draw the bow, and as you swing the *tachi*, your body learns how to do it with ease.

The way to use the *tachi* is not simply to swing it fast. I will touch on this in the second book, the Book of Water. The first rule is to use the *tachi* in open spaces, and the *wakizashi* in confined spaces.

In my school you win with the long *tachi*, you win with the short *wakizashi*.

The important point of my school is not the length of the sword, but that you can win with either one. The advantage of carrying two swords over one becomes clear when one person has to face many, or when you have to fight someone barricaded indoors. There is no need to go into detail here. From one thing you must understand ten thousand. Once you have grasped the essence of military strategy, you can see everything from beginning to end. Keep this fixed firmly in mind.

Understanding the Meaning of Strategy

Among martial artists in general, experts with the *tachi* are referred to as military strategists. In contrast, those who are good with a bow and arrow are called archers; those good with a musket called musketeers; those good with a spear called spearmen; and those good with a halberd called halberdiers.

So it would make sense if the user of a *tachi* was called a *tachi* wielder, and the user of a *wakizashi* was called a *wakizashi* wielder. The bow, musket, spear, and halberd are all tools of the samurai, and all fall within the Way of strategy.

But there is a good reason why only users of the *tachi* are called strategists. The awesomeness of the *tachi* apparently first gave order to the world and provided self-discipline, and thus the *tachi* is the fountainhead of strategy.

If you make the virtues of the *tachi* your own, you can single-handedly defeat 10 opponents. And if one person can defeat 10, then 100 can defeat 1,000, and 1,000 can defeat 10,000. In our school, therefore, there is no difference between one person and 10,000.

As far as the Way is concerned, there are many different types of Ways in the world: the Confucian, the Buddhist, the aesthete, the etiquette master, and the Noh actor, but none of these is part of the Way of the warrior. Without seeking any of these, if you understand the Way of strategy broadly, you will undoubtedly encounter a path that leads to these other Ways. It is important that each and every person earnestly pursue his own Way.

Understanding Your Weapons as a Part of Strategy

In attempting to understand the efficient use of weapons, it can be said that each has its time and occasion for proper use.

The short *wakizashi* is useful in confined spaces and when at close quarters with the enemy.

The long *tachi* is generally useful in any space.

The halberd seems inferior to the spear on the battlefield. The spear is good for offense, the halberd for defense. When two opponents are of equal strength, the spear is somewhat more advantageous. Both spear and halberd depend on the situation. For instance, both suffer in usefulness in confined spaces. The same applies to encirclement. In brief, they are both weapons for use on the battlefield and are necessary for large engagements.

On the other hand, if you practice the use of the spear indoors, you will be distracted by small things and lose sight of the true Way, making the spear useless on the battlefield.

The bow, when employed in an expeditious manner with spearmen or other corps, is useful in battles in the open when advancing or retreating. However, when attacking a castle, or when a great distance separates the forces, the advantages of the bow cannot be brought to bear.

The bow aside, these days many martial arts look spectacular on the surface but have no substance. These arts are merely for show, and when it comes to a fight, they are useless and without effect.

From within the confines of a castle, there is nothing superior to the musket. In fighting out in the open, the musket is prodigiously effective when test-fired before the battle begins. It is much less effective, however, in the midst of a battle. One advantage of the bow is that you can see the flight of the arrow. In contrast, the bullet from a musket cannot be seen, which isn't good at all. This fact should be fully appreciated.

As for horses, it is important they be strong and tireless, without any quirks.

As for battlefield equipment in general, horses should be capable of traveling good distances, the *katana* and *wakizashi* should have sharp cutting edges, the spear and halberd capable of deep penetration, and the bows and muskets should be durable and not easily broken.

You shouldn't grow too attached to any of your equipment. When their time has passed, they are no longer useful.

Without copying others, you should see that your equipment fits you and suits your needs. Whether a commander or a foot soldier, you should not show preference for a special weapon. What is crucial is adapting to immediate needs.

Timing in Strategy

The matter of timing, or rhythm, occurs in any endeavor you might undertake, but particularly in strategy, training in timing is absolutely essential.

Looking around, we see rhythm everywhere, in Noh artists, *gagaku* musicians, and suchlike, where proper timing is essential. In the Way of martial arts, timing can be seen in the shooting of arrows, in the firing of muskets, in horseback riding, and so on. No matter what the art, it cannot turn its back on timing.

Timing even plays a part in matters without a tangible form. From the viewpoint of the samurai, there is the timing involved in serving one's lord and rising in the world, or in coming down in the world, or in hitting it off with someone or not; all of these involve timing.

In the world of business, there is the timing involved in making a fortune or in losing one. Each of these Ways of the world has its own timing. We can see that rhythm is involved in the flourishing and decline of the world.

In strategy, there are also various types of timing. First, you must understand the timing involved in being in harmony with your opponent, and then how to disrupt that harmony. And once that is learned, you must comprehend the timing of the small and the large, the fast and the slow, and in that context, you must know how to establish timing, pause timing, and reverse your opponent's timing back on himself. This is all essential.

In particular, you cannot be a true strategist without a knowledge of reverse timing.

In battle, you must sense the timing of each of your opponents, and then, using a timing totally unexpected by your opponents, you create an invisible timing from a purely intellectual notion and down your opponent.

Every book will contain some special comments on timing. Fix these comments in your mind and train to master them.

If you put into practice, day and night, what I have noted here concerning my school of strategy, you will naturally acquire a broader perspective. Whether involving one person or many, what I have written here for the first time applies to all aspects of strategy as I have taught them heretofore. It is divided up into five books: Earth, Water, Fire, Wind, and Emptiness.

For those who wish to learn the Way of strategy, here is a way to do it.

1. Honestly following the true Way.
2. Train continuously.
3. Come in contact with many and various arts.
4. Know many and various occupations.

5. Distinguish between profit and loss in things.
6. Learn to tell the difference between the true and the false.
7. Sense that which cannot be seen.
8. Pay attention to details.
9. Refrain from engaging in useless activities.

Keep in mind these general points and train hard in the Way of strategy.

Unless you see into the truth behind things from a broad perspective, you cannot hope to become a master of strategy. Once you've mastered the Way, you can single-handedly defeat 20 or 30 opponents. But first you have to fill your spirit with a desire to learn the Way of strategy, and then, if you wholeheartedly apply yourself, you can defeat an opponent with your hands and with your eyes; and if you train hard and gain full freedom of your body, you can win with your body, and finally, if you possess the will to conquer the Way, you can win by spirit alone. Having reached this level, you should never suffer defeat again, regardless of the circumstances.

On the other hand, in the case of strategy involving moving large numbers of people in battle, you win by having capable subordinates, you win by effective handling of people, you win by your ability to govern territory, and you win by being outstanding in your care for the masses and exceptional in your ability to maintain peace and order.

Whatever the opposing Way may be, the Way of strategy means knowing that you cannot be defeated, that your life will be preserved, and you will make a name for yourself.

> Twelfth day, fifth month,
> Shōhō 2 (1645)
> TO: Lord Terao Magonojō
> FROM: Shinmen Musashi

> Fifth day, second month,
> Kanbun 7 (1667)
> TO: Lord Yamamoto Gensuke
> FROM: Terao Yumeyo Katsunobu

The Book of Water

The Book of Water　水の巻

　宮本武蔵が自らの心身の鍛錬法を説いた巻。水を手本として、心は広く真っ直ぐに、姿勢は普通に、太刀は軽く握り、足は自然に動かすことを重視する。構えは有構無構で、相手の内面まで見通す観の目を強くする。

【主な難しい用語や表現】

ページ

29	astray	迷って
30	composure	平常心
	slack	ゆるんだ, だらけた
32	posture	姿勢
	goggle	目をむく
	unprotruding	突き出ていない
	close the wedge	くさびをしめる
	scabbard	鞘
32	parry	かわす, 受け流す
36	traverse	横断する, 横切る
40	crosswise	交差した
42	disposition	配置
43	lax	ゆるい, 手ぬるい
	in disarray	混乱して
44	belatedly	遅れて
47	take a stance	姿勢を取る
48	adhesive	粘着性の
50	tenaciously	執拗に
52	fend off	払いのける, かわす
55	oral transmission	口伝
57	rationale	道理

At the heart of the *Ni Ten Ichi Ryū* school lies the concept of water. The Book of Water will show how to practically utilize this concept by giving a general description of our school.

This subject is filled with fine points, which cannot be set down on paper as easily as one would like. Still, even if description is lacking, in time you should be able to grasp the meaning.

Each and every word written here, each and every letter, should be turned over and over in your mind. A half-hearted reading often leads the reader astray.

And when, concerning the benefits of strategy, I write about one-on-one engagements, you should think of it as applying to engagements of 10,000 against 10,000, grasping it from a broader perspective. This is an essential point.

I should also mention that, with the Way of strategy, straying slightly from the correct path can lead to uncertainty and wandering off the path altogether.

Further, simply reading the words written here is not sufficient to grasp the essence of the Way of strategy.

You should think of this book as a note to yourself—something which you don't merely read or learn from, nor even try to imitate, but as some advantageous points you have discovered, and which you constantly keep in mind and try to improve upon.

The Proper Attitude in Strategy

It is vitally important in the Way of strategy to maintain your composure.

In your daily life, as well as in times of crisis, there should be no change in you; you should look at things directly with an open mind, without being either tense or slack; you should not lean in one direction or another but place your mind in the center; you should not be absorbed by any one thing but move freely with the flow, without interrupting that flow. This is how you must maintain your composure.

In times of quiet, the heart is not quiet; when the action is fast, the heart is not fast; the heart is not overly influenced by action, and action is not overly influenced by the heart; when you are concerned about something, the body is not influenced by that concern; the heart is continually full but not overflowing; outward appearance may appear weak, but the inner heart is strong; and you must not let others see what is in your mind.

Men of small stature must have a thorough understanding of men of large stature; and large men must understand the small.

It is important that both the large and the small have straight hearts and that they be unconcerned about their stature.

The heart should not be cluttered, but must be a wide-open space where you can place your knowledge of things.

Your knowledge of things and your heart must be continually polished and honed. With your knowledge thoroughly honed, you can distinguish between right and wrong, know good from bad, and then experience all the various artistic Ways. And once you get so you are no longer fooled by the people of the world, that fact in itself becomes a wisdom applicable to the Way of strategy. But in the wisdom of the Way of strategy there is something different from the others. On the battlefield, when everything is in violent motion, you must resolutely seek to perfect the Way of strategy and maintain an immovable heart.

Posture in Strategy

Concerning posture, the face should not be turned down, nor should it be turned up, nor inclined to one side or twisted; the eyes should not goggle, nor should there be wrinkles on the forehead or between the eyebrows; the eyeballs should not move and the eyes should be narrowed as if intending not to blink, with a mild expression on one's face, the nose ridge straight and the jaw slightly thrust forward—this is the feeling you should strive for.

The muscle at the back of the neck should consciously be kept straight, the back of the neck firm, and the body from the neck down balanced.

Lower both shoulders, keep the back muscles straight, the buttocks unprotruding and firmness in both legs from the knees down to the toes, with the belly thrust out so you are not bent forward at the waist. There is a saying, "Close the wedge," which means to hold down the scabbard of the *wakizashi* with the belly, ensuring like a wedge that the sash doesn't become loose.

Overall, it is important in strategy for the posture adopted in everyday life to be the posture adopted in battle, and the posture adopted in battle to be the posture of everyday life. This should not be forgotten.

Use of the Eyes in Strategy

The use of the eyes requires that they be used largely and broadly.

There are two Chinese characters with which to write "see." In one the eyes are strong, in the other weak.

In battle it is important to quickly discern things in the distance, and to see things up close as if further away. Knowing that what you see is indeed the enemy's sword, you must not in the least be absorbed by that sword. Adjust as necessary.

The use of the eyes is the same for individual fighting as it is for large-scale fighting. Without moving the eyes, you must be able to see to both sides.

This cannot be easily accomplished when hard pressed. You must fix in your mind what is written here and train yourself to make constant use of the eyes in this way, assuring that no one can read your eyes in any situation.

How to Hold the *Tachi*

The *tachi* should be held so that the thumb and index finger feel slightly uplifted, the middle finger not tight but not loose, and the ring finger and small finger slightly tight. There should be no play or looseness in the palm of the hand.

When you pick up your sword, it should be with the intent of cutting down your opponent.

And when you cut your opponent, there is no change in the state of the hand, which is holding the sword without tensing up. When parrying the opponent's sword, receiving it, striking it, or applying pressure, only the thumb and the index figure exhibit some change. In any case, you have to take up your sword with the intent of cutting down your enemy.

Whether in test cutting, in an earnest bout, or in an attempt to cut someone down, there is no change in the hand.

Overall, in the handling of the sword and in the

use of the hand, tenseness is not good. To be tense means to die. To be relaxed and loose means to live. You should keep this firmly in mind.

On Footwork

The movement of the feet is done by slightly uplifting the toes and pushing off forcefully with the heels.

Depending on the situation, there is some difference in the length of stride and the speed of movement, but fundamentally the movement of the feet is done as in ordinary walking.

Jumping movement, floating movement, and heavy movement are not good.

In the Way of strategy, ying-yang footwork is favored. This means never moving only one foot, but whether in moving forward to cut, or moving back, or receiving the opponent's blade, both left and right feet should be moved. Be careful that you don't move only one foot at a time.

The Five Stances

The five stances, or guard positions, are upper level,

middle level, lower level, right underarm, and left underarm.

The purpose of all five is to cut down your opponent.

There are no other stances besides these five. In all five, you should not think of stances but of cutting your opponent.

The size of the stance, whether large or small, depends on what feels right for the situation. The upper, middle, and lower levels are the norm. The left and right underarm stances are adaptations. They are used when there is no space above and one of the sides is obstructed. Whether to adopt one or the other depends on the place.

The Way of strategy's constant view is that the middle level stance is the most important. Think of this in terms of a large-scale engagement. The middle level is equivalent to the commander who sits in the middle of his troops. This should not be forgotten.

The Path of the *Tachi*

Concerning the course traversed by the *tachi*, if you have a good understanding of the path it will take, you can wield it with freedom, even though using only two fingers.

If you try to swing the *tachi* too fast, you will mistake its path and mishandle the swing. You can swing the *tachi* well if you wield it with a feeling of calmness. However, if you try to swing it quickly as you would a fan or a short sword, you will mistake the path of its passage and do it badly.

This is the same as swinging wildly with a short sword. In that way, there is no way you can cut down anyone. If you swing down with a *tachi*, you have to do so in a way that it can be easily raised up. If you swing to the side, the *tachi* should be brought back on an easy path. However, in whatever way you do it, the elbows should be fully extended and the swing strong; this is the Way of the *tachi*.

If you learn the five fundamental forms of my school, the path of the *tachi* will become fixed, and swinging will become much easier. Train hard.

The First of the Five Fundamental Forms

The first form takes the middle level stance.

When you meet an enemy and have the tip of your *tachi* pointed at his face, and the enemy attacks, you deflect his *tachi* to the right.

If he attacks again, you swing down with the tip of the sword and maintain a static position with the sword down, and if your opponent attacks again, you swing up, aiming at his arms. This is the first form.

However, it is not enough just to write down and read these five fundamental forms. It is necessary to actually pick up your sword and practice. As far as the five paths of the *tachi* are concerned, if you study the Way of my school, you will come to see what paths the enemy's *tachi* will take in what circumstances.

That is precisely why my *Nitō* school teaches that there are no more than five stances. Train hard.

The Second of the Five Fundamental Forms

The second of the ways to wield a *tachi* requires the upper level stance, and when an enemy attacks you, you immediately attack back.

If you have missed your mark, leave the *tachi* in its downward position, and swing up if your opponent attacks again. If another attack comes, the same approach applies.

This fundamental form contains many things

requiring care and matters concerning timing. But if you practice these fundamentals in the Way of my school, you will learn the finer points of the five fundamental forms and will prevail in any situation. Practice is all-important.

The Third of the Five Fundamental Forms

Third is waiting in a lower level stance, with swords hanging down, and swinging up at the enemy's arms as he attacks.

When you try to hit his arms, he may try to attack again. You ward this off, and pausing a moment after the enemy's attack, respond by an attack on his upper arm.

In the lower level stance, you stop the enemy as he makes his attack.

When studying the paths of the *tachi*, the lower level stance must be learned, whether at the beginning or later. Practice hard with a *tachi*.

The Fourth of the Fundamental Forms

In the fourth form, the *tachi* is held horizontally in

the left underarm position. When the enemy attacks, you strike up at his hands.

When striking from below, if the enemy attempts to parry, receive the path of his sword as if striking at his hands. Aiming above your own shoulder, strike diagonally.

This is how the *tachi* is swung. If the enemy should continue to attack, this is the way to win, receiving the path of his sword. Examine this well.

The Fifth of the Fundamental Forms

The fifth approach calls for the *tachi* to be held crosswise in front of the right underarm, and in response to the enemy's attack, swung upward diagonally to the upper level position; the *tachi* then cuts the opponent from straight above.

This method is undertaken to understand the path of the *tachi*. If you wield your *tachi* as described in this approach, you will get so that you can handle a heavy *tachi* freely.

I will not go into detail about these five forms. You should learn the basics of our school's usage of the *tachi*, have a general understanding of timing, and in order to follow the movement of the enemy's *tachi*, practice daily to perfect your skills in accordance with these five fundamental forms.

In combat this will allow you to follow the path of the *tachi*, anticipate your opponent's intent, and win by using various types of timing. Understand this well.

The Stance of No Stance

The stance of no stance—that is, there is a stance but at the same time there is no stance—means that while it is true that the *tachi* should not be forced into a fixed form, it is also true that we have five fundamental stances.

The *tachi* should be held according to how the enemy is encountered, the place, the circumstances, and what is the easiest way to cut down the enemy in a particular situation.

Depending on circumstances, an upper level stance can become middle level by slightly lowering the sword, and a middle level can become an upper level by slightly raising it, according to your judgment. Depending on the situation, the lower level stance can become middle level by slightly raising the *tachi*. Both underarm stances can become middle or lower stances, depending on their exact position.

In the end, there is a stance, but it is not a fixed stance.

Most important of all is that the purpose of taking a sword in hand is to cut down the enemy. Remember that if an enemy attacks and you receive, deflect, make contact, persevere, and touch, you should think of all these as opportunities to cut your enemy.

If you are consciously aware of receiving the *tachi*, of deflecting, hitting, persevering, and touching it, you won't be able to cut the enemy.

It is important to remember that all this presents an opportunity for cutting the enemy. Fix this very firmly in your mind.

In large-scale military strategy, the disposition of troops is done for the opportunities it presents to win. It is not good to concentrate on only one thing. Adapting to the situation is needed.

The Single-Timing Attack of an Enemy

With respect to timing, there is one attack called a single-timing attack, in which the distance between your opponent and yourself is one sword length. Before your opponent is mentally ready, and without moving yourself physically or mentally, there is a moment when you can attack your opponent in a flash.

Before he can think of retreating, evading, or cutting, you attack. This is single timing. Learn this timing and practice closing the distance and cutting your opponent.

Double Timing

In double timing, when you attack, your opponent quickly retreats and deflects your *tachi*. You pretend to follow in attack, and immediately after your opponent wards off your blow again, there is a moment when he grows lax. It is this moment you use to instantly attack, cutting as your opponent retreats in disarray. This is called double timing.

You will probably not do well just from reading this description, but with the proper instruction you will be able to get it.

The No Thought No Form Cut

Your opponent is ready to attack, and you are ready to attack. The body is prepared to attack, and the heart is ready. At that point, without you realizing it, your hand belatedly appears out of Emptiness and strikes strongly.

This is known as the "no thought no form" cut. It is an extremely important means of attack. It is often seen in combat. Learn it well and practice hard.

The Flowing Water Cut

This cut occurs when you are fighting on equal terms with an opponent and he tries to retreat quickly, to disengage quickly, and to deflect your *tachi* quickly. You respond by adopting an attitude that enlarges yourself both physically and mentally, swinging largely and strongly, extremely slowly like a slow flowing river, swinging slower than the movement of your body.

If you learn this, it will certainly make fighting much easier. In this situation, it is extremely important to observe the appearance of your opponent.

The Chance Cut

When you attack and your opponent tries to stop the attack by parrying your blow, you cut at both his hands and his feet with one swing.

By swinging the *tachi* on one path, you can hit wherever you want. This is the chance cut.

This cut should be learned, for it is often experienced. By repeated practice you will understand it.

The Flintstone Cut

This strike occurs when your opponent's *tachi* and your *tachi* are entangled, and you strike your opponent strongly without raising your sword in the least.

You must strengthen your hands and feet, and strike quickly using the hands, feet, and body.

This technique cannot be performed without repeated practice. But hard training will enable you to deliver a strong strike.

The Falling Leaves Cut

This cut involves knocking down your opponent's sword and detaching it from him.

When your opponent stands in front of you with his *tachi* and is ready to strike or hit or receive, you strongly strike his sword with the "no thought no form" cut or the flintstone cut. Entangling his sword so that it cannot be easily extracted, you lower the tip of your sword and strike. Invariably you will knock the sword from his hand.

With training, it is easy to knock down a sword. Practice hard.

The Sword Follows the Body

This could also be called "the body follows the sword."

In general, when attacking an opponent, the body and *tachi* do not move at the same time. Depending on your opponent's approach, first you take your stance, and quite unrelated to that, the *tachi* proceeds to strike your opponent.

Or, on the other hand, the body does not move,

and only the *tachi* moves. But by and large, the body takes a stance, followed by an attack with the *tachi*.

This point should be studied, and you should practice this movement.

To Strike and to Hit

To strike and to hit are two different things. Regardless of the nature of the fight, to strike means to consciously cut your opponent.

To make a hit means to unintentionally strike your advancing opponent, and even if he should die from the force of the blow, it is still considered an inadvertent hit.

In other words, to strike means to attack consciously. Whether it is the hands or the feet, a hit is still inadvertent. To make a hit, it is first necessary to collide with one's opponent. After making bodily contact, then you strike forcefully. The initial collision is merely to feel out your opponent. If you practice hard, you will see that striking and hitting are entirely different. Adapt as you learn.

The Monkey's Body

The monkey's body refers to a short-handed monkey and warns us not to be too quick with our hands.

You approach your opponent, and without making an attempt to strike, you move in very close before your opponent has a chance to strike.

If you attempt to strike yourself, your bodies will move apart. So instead of doing that, you move in quickly with your whole body.

If you are within reaching distance of each other, it is not difficult to move in close. Work to understand this.

The Adhesive Body

The adhesive body means to stick bodily close to your opponent's body and not come apart.

When you move in close like this, you have to press up against your opponent with head, body, and legs.

It often happens that the head and legs arrive first and the body is left behind. You have to force your whole body up against your opponent's without the smallest gap. Learn this well.

Comparing Heights

This means when pressing up close to your opponent, you must not shrink back in any way. You must stretch out your legs, torso, and neck to their fullest extent, pressing your opponent hard. With your head on the same level as his, and stretching out to your full height as you bear down on him, you must take the attitude that even if you were to compare heights, you would win.

This is an important point, which you should adapt to the situation.

The Sticky Sword

When you confront the attack of your opponent, receiving his *tachi* with yours, you push your *tachi* up against his so that they stick together while you push in with your body.

Stickiness here means seeing that the *tachi* don't separate, pushing physically in but not too hard.

When you push up against your opponent and

tenaciously keep the swords together, you can do this quietly.

Being stuck together, as compared with being entangled, is strong while entanglement is weak. Understand this.

The Body Strike

The body strike is when you enter your opponent's most immediate space and make physical contact with your body.

Turn your head slightly to one side, thrust out your left shoulder, and hit your opponent with it in the chest.

When you do this, do it as strongly as possible, with force and momentum. If you learn how to execute this properly, you can develop the power to send your opponent flying four or five meters.

You will get so that you can hit your opponent so hard that it could be life threatening. Practice hard.

Three Ways to Parry

The first of the three ways to parry occurs when

you enter your opponent's territory and he cuts at you. In response, you thrust your *tachi* toward your opponent's eyes and deflect his *tachi* off to your right.

The second occurs when your opponent attacks with his sword, and you parry it by thrusting at his right eye, sandwiching his head with your two swords.

The third occurs when your opponent attacks and you engage with your short sword. Without paying much attention to the parrying *tachi*, you engage by thrusting your shorter sword at your opponent's face.

These are the three ways of parrying. It is important to use your left hand as if it were a fist being powerfully thrust at your opponent. This requires considerable practice.

Thrusting at the Face

This means that whenever in close combat, you should always be mentally ready to thrust at your opponent's face with the tip of your sword, making use of any gap between your *tachi* and that of your opponent.

If you do this, your opponent's head and body

will arch back, providing an opening to win. Adapt this to the situation.

In the midst of a fight, if your opponent arches back, that decides the match. That is why thrusting at the face is so important. Make use of this in your practice and understand it well.

Stabbing at the Heart

This means that when fighting in places where it is hard to strike because there is little room above and the sides are cramped, you thrust at your opponent.

As for the timing of fending off you opponent's *tachi* when he attacks, you show the ridge of your sword directly to your opponent, drawing it back so that the point of the sword is unwavering, and then thrust at his chest.

When you are exhausted or your blade has grown dull, this technique is widely used. Use your judgment.

The Hey-You Thrust

This technique occurs as you attack an opponent who is being pushed back and attempts to counter.

Here you thrust up from below and strike him on the return blow. All this is done with fast timing. Remember to strike with "Hey you!" timing. "Hey!" for the up-thrust, and "You!" for the cut. This timing is often encountered in fast fighting.

It is important in this technique to raise the tip of the sword with the idea that you will thrust at your opponent, and then lifting the sword, bring it down with full force. Practice hard and reach an understanding of this technique.

Parrying with the Flat of the Sword

This means that in exchanging blows with your opponent and the timing becomes progressively worse, you slap his sword when he attacks with the flat of yours and then strike.

Slapping does not mean hitting hard, nor does it mean to block. It means hitting in proportion to the opponent's blow. But as soon as you have slapped you must strike.

The point is that by slapping you take the initiative, and when you strike, you further take the initiative. Even if your opponent strikes hard, you shouldn't lose momentum if your timing is right and you have a little understanding of the technique. Practice this and understand it.

Engaging with Many Opponents

This refers to one person engaging many.

Draw your short *wakizashi* and your long *tachi* and let them hang down at your sides, spread left and right. Your opponents will come from many directions, but you should force them back in one direction.

When the attack comes, see who is going to attack first and confront that person, watching the movement of the whole group and noting their positions. Using both swords, you suddenly cut, swinging with both left and right swords.

It is not good to pause after striking. You immediately take up a defensive stance with both swords at your sides. When the enemy attacks, you cut your way into their midst, pushing them back and cutting them down as they come forward.

Using various methods, you herd your opponents in one direction, like a school of fish, and when their formation has become jumbled, you cut into their midst.

When your opponents are many, confronting them head-on is generally not the thing to do. And if you wait for your opponents to come to you, you lose the initiative and the chance for success.

You should know the timing of your opponents' movements, and you can win if you know their weakness. If you learn how to get your numerous opponents gathered together and drive them at the right moment, you can fight ten or twenty opponents as easily as one. Practice hard and learn this.

The Principle of Combat

Through the principles of combat, you will come to understand the ways of winning with the *tachi* in the Way of strategy.

I cannot go into detail here. You must practice and understand this way of winning. All of the Way of strategy is comparable to a *tachi* that records the truth. This teaching is an oral transmission.

The Single Strike

It is perfectly possible to win with one strike of the

sword. If you practice this seriously, you will be able to win at your will using the Way of strategy. Practice hard.

Oral Transmission

Oral transmission means receiving by word of mouth the teachings of *Ni Ten Ichi Ryū* and passing them on. These teachings are for the purpose of acquiring the Way of strategy.

I have recorded here a general outline of *Ni Ten Ichi Ryū* sword fighting. Military strategy is to know how to be victorious by means of a *tachi*. First, you must know the five stances and the five fundamental forms, learn the path of the *tachi* and gain freedom of movement, be mentally quick and understand timing, and gain a natural mastery of the handling of the *tachi*. As you gain freedom of movement with both body and legs, you can win against one person or against two. Then as you understand both the good and the bad of strategy and practice according to each and every item recorded here, you will engage in combat and gradually begin to understand the principles of the Way of strategy.

You are always being mindful of the Way, but

you don't hurry. As time affords, you learn with your body the important points. You engage in combat without choosing your opponents, learn to read your opponent's mind, and proceed one step at a time on a long journey.

Without being hurried, you realize that putting the Way into practice is the role of a samurai. Today you defeat the person who was you yesterday. Tomorrow you defeat someone who is even less skillful, and next you will defeat an opponent who is stronger than you. Thinking in this way, you discipline yourself according to what is written here, being careful not to be distracted.

No matter how powerful an opponent you defeat, it is not the true Way if it goes against these teachings.

If you grasp these principles, you can understand the rationale of the Way, and you will be able to defeat dozens of opponents single-handedly.

Beyond that, with the wisdom of the Way of the sword, you will understand the Way of strategy whether you are confronted by many opponents or a single one. It may take a thousand days to temper your skills and ten thousand to forge them. Keep this in mind.

Twelfth day, fifth month,
Shōhō 2 (1645)
TO: Lord Terao Magonojō
FROM: Shinmen Musashi

Fifth day, second month,
Kanbun 7 (1667)
TO: Lord Yamamoto Gensuke
FROM: Terao Yumeyo Katsunobu

The Book of Fire

The Book of Fire　火_かの巻

　宮本武蔵が戦闘の戦術や戦略を説いた巻。戦いを火の勢いに例えて、相手の状況や心理を見極め、有利な環境や先手を取ることを重視する。相手の調子を狂わせたり、行き詰まったら心機一転したりすることも大切とする。

【主な難しい用語や表現】

ページ

63	unobstructed	邪魔のない
	seat of honor	上席
	deprive	奪う，取り上げる
65	leeway	余裕
	falter	怯む
66	lead someone around by the nose	
		（人）を思うままに操る
67	grappling	組み技
	nip ~ in the bud	～の芽を摘む，未然に防ぐ
	make a plaything	思うがままに翻弄する
68	tail wind	追い風
69	ride out the crisis	危機を乗り切る
70	trample	踏みつける
	all-out attack	総攻撃
71	recoup	盛り返す
77	exasperated	憤慨して，いら立って
	nip and tuck	五分五分で
78	stagnate	停滞する
79	protruding	突き出ている
81	before-after shout	先後の声（勝ちを示すかけ声）
82	to smithereens	木っ端みじんに
	in one fell swoop	一挙に
86	hilt	（剣の）つか

In the *Nitō Ichi Ryū* school, fighting is compared to fire, so we will discuss battle in the Book of Fire.

In the world at large, strategy is broken down into ridiculously trivial points, including measurements of the wrist or the elbows. Such people learn how to wield a bamboo sword fractionally faster or how to move their feet or hands. And they want to learn such things as quickly as possible.

On the other hand, in our strategy, in which we engage numerous times in fights with our lives on the line, we know the way of life and death, appreciate the path the sword traverses, know the strengths and weaknesses of our opponents' swords, learn the movements of the sword's ridge, and train ourselves to cut down our opponent. For us, such trivialities are not worth considering.

Furthermore, in a life or death struggle, our Way of strategy is to build a solid path to victory whether fighting one against five or one against ten. The reason one can defeat five is not very different from a thousand defeating ten thousand. You should give this serious consideration.

Having said that, it is impossible in your daily practice to assemble 1,000 or 10,000 people for instructive purposes. What you can do single-handedly, taking *tachi* in hand, is to fathom your opponent's strategy, see through his strengths and weaknesses, and, making use of the resources of the Way of strategy, perfect the means of defeating 10,000 opponents and become a master of the Way, acquiring my school's Way of strategy and seeing into its essence.

Moreover, pledging in your heart to acquire the Way, you discipline yourself in the morning and train yourself in the evening. After you have thoroughly polished your skills, you will be able to move with perfect freedom, having in the course of nature acquired what is difficult to acquire. It is precisely by gaining this mysterious power that the samurai gains the spirit of our Way of strategy.

The Matter of Place

Be aware of your position. First, keep the sun at your back. Take your stance with the sun behind you. Should you be in a place where you cannot put the sun at your back, make it so that it is on your right side.

Needless to say, if you are indoors, keep the light behind you or on your right side. To ensure that your rear is unobstructed, position yourself with a wide space on your left side and a narrow one on your right. If the enemy can be seen, keep any fire behind you and any lighting on your right side, as mentioned above.

In order to look down upon your opponent, it is best to position yourself on a slight elevation. If you are in a formal room, take the seat of honor as being such an elevation. When the fighting starts and you are pursuing your opponent, drive him to your left. See to it that awkward positions are to the rear of your opponent and drive him toward those positions.

When your opponent is in an uncomfortable place, don't give him time to think or look around. If in a room, drive him toward thresholds, doors, shutters, verandas, and such, or drive him toward pillars and so on, attacking with the thought that you will deprive him of any place to settle.

In any case, when pursuing your opponent, drive him toward places with bad footing or obstacles. Whatever kind of place you are in, remember to make the best of its features. Remember that victory is achieved utilizing the nature of the place. Understand this and practice it.

Three Ways of Taking the Initiative

The first way of taking the initiative is to attack first. The second is for your opponent to attack first. The third is for both you and your opponent to attack at the same time.

There are no other ways of taking the initiative, regardless of the nature of the fight. If, depending on which of the three you choose, you are assured victory, then initiative would be the most important strategy in our Way.

There are many things that can be said about the finer points of initiative, but there is no meaning in going into finer detail if you can win by choosing one of the three on the basis of the situation, reading the heart of your opponent, and making your decision based on the resources of our Way of strategy.

The first initiative, as mentioned above, is to be the first to attack. In your attack, you should remain calm but engage with blinding speed.

The movement of your body should be strong

and rapid, but in your heart there should be some leeway. Or again, this is also a possibility: your heart is extremely strong, your footwork is just a little faster than normal, and as you approach your opponent you suddenly burst out with a violent attack. Or in another possibility, you keep your heart calm, attack with the same energy from beginning to end, and win by maintaining the same strong heart.

In the second initiative, when the enemy attacks, you don't engage him at all and pretend to be very weak. As he closes with you, you come out much stronger and fall upon him, and when you see him falter, you go in for a strong win. Or when your opponent attacks, you also come out strong, wait for the moment when his timing changes, and go on to win.

In the third initiative, when your opponent attacks quickly, you respond calmly but strongly, and when he closes with you, you abruptly change your stance. This causes him to falter, which is when you immediately go in for a strong win. Or, alternatively, when the enemy attacks calmly, you attack with a little speed, as if your body were floating, and after some pushing and shoving while your opponent draws near, you wait for the right moment and attack with strength, bringing the enemy down.

All of this cannot be written down and explained in detail. Following these notes, adapt to the circumstances.

These three ways of taking the initiative depend on time and circumstance, and while you cannot always expect to be the first to attack following rational principles, it is better, if possible, to attack first and throw the enemy into confusion. By means of the resources available in the Way of strategy, be confident of your ability to win and practice accordingly.

Holding Down the Pillow

Holding down the pillow means to prevent someone from raising their head.

In the Way of strategy, it is not good to be led around by the nose and to lose the initiative. Whatever it takes, you want to have complete control over your opponent's movements.

This is the way you think, and your opponent is thinking in the same way, so you will not be able to take the initiative unless you can predict his movements.

In the Way of strategy, you must prevent your

opponent from striking, stop him from thrusting, and block any attempt at grappling. Holding down the pillow means that you engage the enemy with a strategic plan in mind and that you know what your opponent is thinking before he acts. If he is going to strike, you must nip the action in the bud, preventing any follow-up action.

For example, if your opponent is going to *engage*, you want to prevent it at the letter *e*. If he is going to *jump*, you want to prevent it at the letter *j*. And if *cut*, prevent it at *c*. This is exactly the same thinking. And when your opponent tries some technique on you, you let him do what is harmless, but prevent what is harmful. This type of prevention lies at the heart of the Way of strategy.

Thinking constantly that you must prevent what your opponent is doing is a defensive act. First, while following the path of strategy in whatever you do and in executing your techniques, you must nip in the bud any harmful techniques that have popped into your opponent's head. Making a plaything of one's opponent in this way is the work of someone who is well acquainted with the Way of strategy. This is the fruit of discipline and training. Understanding holding down the pillow is extremely important.

Crossing the Water

This means, for example, to cross a narrow strait you have come up against, or it may mean crossing an open sea of over a hundred kilometers.

And when people cross from one end of life to the other, they may encounter as many troubles as in crossing an ocean.

Concerning the route, you know the dangerous crossings, you know the position of your ship, you have read the good and bad signs for that day, and you realize there will be no companion ship. You understand that you must adjust according to circumstance, that you may have a side wind, that you may have a tail wind, or that the wind may change altogether and force you to row the last few kilometers to reach the harbor. It is with such feelings that you manage your boat and set out to cross the water.

If you make your way through life with this in mind, and a crisis occurs, you can think of it as making a difficult crossing.

In the case of fighting according to the Way of strategy, the idea of making a crossing is important. With a good notion of the capabilities of your enemy, and knowing your own strengths, you size up the situation and make your difficult crossing.

This is the same as a ship's captain steering his boat through a dangerous passage. If you successfully make the crossing and ride out the crisis, the rest is simple. Once across, the power is on your side and you have the upper hand. If you can do that, then you can generally win.

Whether fighting one-on-one or in a large-scale battle, it is important to maintain the notion of making a dangerous crossing. Look into this carefully.

Know the Situation

To know the situation in a large-scale battle according to the Way of strategy means to know if enemy morale is high or low, to know the number of its forces, to determine its strength in its present position, to decide how you can maneuver the number of troops you have, to determine how you can be sure to win according to the principles of the Way of strategy, and to foresee how you can take the initiative and win.

In the case of one-on-one engagements, determine the school of your opponent, know his character, attack him in unexpected ways after seeing what his strengths and weaknesses are, and when you have judged the variability in his condition and the nature of his timing, take the initiative.

If you make free use of the Way of strategy and see into the heart of your opponent, there are many ways to achieve victory. Study and adapt.

Trampling on a Sword

The notion of trampling on a sword is exclusive to the Way of strategy.

In large-scale battles with bows and muskets, the enemy first employs these weapons and then follows with an all-out attack. But bows and muskets are not useful in hand-to-hand fighting because the former has to be restrung and the latter reloaded.

When the enemy is using bows and muskets, it is best to attack as quickly as possible. If you do this, the enemy has no time to restring or reload. When the enemy attacks in this way, accept these conditions and crush their attack underfoot.

In one-on-one fights, if you respond every time the enemy strikes with his *tachi*, the timing becomes a monotonous ta-dum ta-dum, preventing you from fighting well. When the enemy strikes with his *tachi*, you should strike strongly back as he makes his move, as if trampling on his sword, and prevent him from making a following move.

To trample means not only to trample with the feet. You also trample with your body and your heart. Of course, you trample with your sword, too. With this strong feeling you make it difficult for your opponent to make a follow-up attack. This is taking the initiative.

It does not mean to collide with your body at the moment he attacks. You should feel as though you were going to cling fast to him after he moves. Look carefully into this.

Collapsing

At one time or another, everything can collapse.

When something goes amiss, houses collapse, our bodies fall into collapse, and our enemies collapse.

In war it is essential that you grasp the instant of your enemy's collapse and that you attack immediately. If you miss that instant, the enemy may recoup his forces.

When fighting one-on-one, there are sometimes

signs that your opponent has lost his timing and is ready to collapse. If you don't catch these signs, your opponent may recover, recoup his position, and gain the advantage.

You need to see the first sign of collapse, attack it, and press so hard that your opponent can't recover.

At that moment, you must attack all at once, with full strength, and force him back with strong strikes so that he can't recoup his position. You must thoroughly understand the matter of forcing your opponent back with strong blows. If you don't strongly force him back, you may be too late. Study and adapt.

Becoming the Enemy

This means: What would I be thinking if I were the enemy? It is generally thought that a burglar hiding out in a house is a strong individual. But from the viewpoint of the burglar, all the world is his enemy, which is why he is hiding out in the house, and so he is undoubtedly feeling terribly desperate.

You can compare that person with a pheasant, which a hawk is going to kill. You should understand this and adapt it.

In large-scale battles, you may overestimate the strength of the enemy and grow wary and overly cautious. But if you have a sufficient number of troops, understand the principles of strategy, and know the way to defeat the enemy, there is no need to worry.

Also when one-on-one, put yourself strategically in the place of the enemy.

If the enemy realizes that his opponent is knowledgeable in strategy, is familiar with the principles of sword fighting, and is a master of the Way, he is most likely thinking that he doesn't have a chance. This is something you should be fully aware of.

Letting Go of Four Hands

This refers to a state when you and your opponent are fighting it out using the same techniques, locked hand in hand, so to speak.

When you are fighting it out in this way and you find that you are incapable of doing anything different, you have to abandon the present state and switch to a more favorable one that allows you to win.

In large-scale engagements, sometimes you get locked inextricably in battle with the enemy, there is no progress, and lives are lost. It is vital that you remove yourself from that condition as soon as possible, surprise the enemy with an unexpected move, and win.

In one-on-one combat, if you find yourself getting locked in, it is crucial that you at once change your tactics and try various courses of action to bring about a win.

Use good judgment in this.

Moving Your Shadow

Moving your shadow refers to times when you cannot read the enemy's mind.

In battle, when it proves impossible to know how your opponent will move, make a strong feint at him and see what his tactical reaction is.

Once you know the enemy's strategy, it will work to your advantage and make winning easier.

In individual combat, when your opponent assumes a stance with his *tachi* held back or to one side, make a sudden attack, and your opponent's intentions will be revealed by the movement of his sword. Once you have seen that, you must make use of it and go on to win.

If you are lax, you will miss your chance. Observe well.

Suppressing the Shadow

Suppressing the shadow refers to occasions when you can see that the enemy is about to attack.

In battle, when the enemy is ready to make a strong attack, you stifle his tactic and show that you are going to react forcefully. The enemy is pressed back by your attack and becomes unsure of himself. That's when you change your tactics, and without the slightest hesitation take the initiative and go on to win.

In one-on-one combat, seize the right timing to threaten the intent indicated by the enemy, and prevent him from carrying out his intended action. When he gives up the action, you take this as an opportunity for victory and seize the initiative. Work hard on this.

Being Contagious

Some things can spread from one person to another.

Sleepiness can spread to another person. So can a yawn. Even time is contagious.

In battles involving large-scale strategy, when you see that the enemy is faltering and uncertain, you pretend to be perfectly at ease and unaffected by the enemy's situation. This air of ease will spread to the enemy, who will become lax.

Once you see that this mood has spread to the enemy, you attack strongly and swiftly without a moment's thought and seize the chance for victory.

In individual combat, when you appear perfectly relaxed and at ease, the enemy grows lax, and you attack strongly and swiftly and go on to win.

There is something similar to this called intoxication. First, you make your opponent grow lax. Second, you make him grow nervous. Third, you make him timid. Take all this and work on it.

How to Exasperate the Enemy

There are times when the enemy becomes

exasperated. First is when the battle is nip and tuck. Second is when the enemy has overreached himself. Third is when something unexpected occurs. Give this much thought.

In battle, it is important to exasperate the enemy—that is, to irritate him or anger him. Make a violent attack just when the enemy is not expecting it, and while he is thoroughly befuddled, seize this chance to take the initiative and win.

In one-on-one engagements, first seem perfectly at ease and relaxed, and then strongly attack in a split second. Following up on your opponent's confused movements, you seize the moment without the slightest pause and carry on to win. This is crucial. You must learn this thoroughly.

To Frighten the Enemy

To feel frightened is not unusual.

What frightens us is the unexpected. In battle strategy, the enemy can be frightened by what cannot be seen. The enemy can be frightened by a cry or by making a small number of troops appear to be a large one.

Or he can be frightened by a sudden attack from

the side. There are many ways to put fear into the enemy. You seize this moment of fear as your chance for victory and go on to win.

In the strategy of individual combat, you can frighten with your body, with your *tachi*, and with your voice.

You can alarm your opponent by an abrupt, unexpected attack, and as he falters, you seize the moment and go on to victory. Understand this thoroughly.

Mixing with the Enemy

This refers to a situation in which you are fighting at close quarters, with both sides contending equally. When the fight begins to stagnate, you mix in with the enemy, and in their midst you find a chance for victory.

Both in large-scale strategy and in one-on-one strategy, when the two sides of the fight are clearly distinguishable, there are times when the contenders cannot produce a victor.

At such times, you quickly mix in with the enemy, make enemy and friend indistinguishable, find advantageous conditions there, realize the way to victory, and gain a strong win.

Attacking the Corners

This means that when facing a formidable enemy, it is not easy to attack head-on.

In battle, after observing the enemy's numbers, attack a protruding corner and seize the chance for victory. When that corner disappears, all else becomes weaker.

It is essential, as the enemy gets weaker, to continue attacking the corners, grasping the chance for victory.

Also when fighting a single opponent, if you damage the corners of his body, the whole person weakens and collapses, making it easier to achieve victory.

Examine this thoroughly and know the way to victory.

To Bewilder the Enemy

This means to keep the enemy from remaining calm

and collected.

In large-scale strategy, you first understand the enemy's thinking at this stage of the fighting, and then using the resources of the Way of strategy, you keep the enemy guessing about various factors: here or there, how or when, fast or slow. Then as the enemy becomes thoroughly flustered, you seize the moment of victory and go on to win.

In one-on-one strategy, seizing the proper moment, you vary your techniques, or you feint a strike or feint a stab, or make it seem you are going to get in close. As soon as you see your opponent falter, you waste no time in going for a victory.

This is the essence of battle. Learn it well.

Three Kinds of Shouts

This refers to the three kinds of shouts that occur at the beginning, middle, and end of a confrontation.

At times it is important to shout. A shout produces energy. When you shout at the time of a fire or into the wind and waves, you are showing the force of your being.

In battlefield strategy, the shout at the beginning of the fight should be loud enough to intimidate the enemy. The shout in the middle of fighting should be low, coming from your depths. After achieving victory, the shout should be loud and forceful. These are the three kinds of shouts.

To move your opponent in one-on-one combat, you feint a strike and shout "*Ei!*," following this with a strike from your *tachi*.

The shout given after having defeated your opponent is to announce your victory. It is called the "before-after shout."

There is no loud shout accompanying a strike with the *tachi*. If you shout in the midst of the fighting, it should be to help your timing, and it should be low.

Learn this thoroughly.

Tacking into the Wind

This refers to large-scale battles in which two numerous forces are confronting each other. When the opposing force seems formidable, you attack one front at a time, and when that front seems on the verge of collapse, you disengage yourself and attack another strong front. This is called tacking. It means you attack in a zigzag pattern.

When you are alone and facing numerous opponents, you should fight with this in mind. Without becoming fixated on one front, you quickly move here and there, attacking the strong areas. You grasp your opponents' rhythm, improve your timing as you zigzag right and left, and go on attacking as you watch your opponents' movements. You should be fully aware of your opponents' overall condition, and when you attack, you shouldn't hold back in the least but strongly go for the winning chance.

When closing with a strong opponent, you should attack with the same mentality. You shouldn't hold back, but tack into the wind. Understand this well.

Crushing

Crushing means, for instance, when you think your opponent is weak and you feel strong, you crush your opponent in one fell swoop.

In battle strategy, when you have confirmed that the enemy is small in number, or is faltering and weak even if numerous, you attack relentlessly from the very beginning and smash the opposing force to smithereens. This is what crushing means.

If your all-out attack lacks force, the enemy may recover. You should understand crushing as being similar to holding something in your hand and squeezing it with all your might.

In one-on-one strategy, if you realize that your opponent is inexperienced, that his timing is off, or that he has lost momentum, it is essential that you attack in one fell swoop, without the slightest pause and without meeting your opponent's eyes.

This must be done so that there is no possibility of him recovering. Understand this well.

Changing from Mountain to Sea

The spirit of changing from mountain to sea means that when confronting an opponent, you should avoid frequently repeating the same thing.

While it might be unavoidable to repeat something twice, you shouldn't do it three times. Let's say you try a technique once and it fails; you try it again and still it isn't effective. Then you try something entirely different, hoping to catch him off balance, and if that doesn't work, you try something different again.

That is, if the enemy is thinking of a mountain,

you hit him with the sea, and if he is thinking of the sea, you hit him with a mountain, all in accordance with the principles of strategy. Understand this well.

Knocking the Bottom Out

When confronting an enemy, it may appear that you have won by seizing the moment through the use of the Way of strategy, but the enemy still hasn't lost the will to fight, only superficially appearing that way; in his heart he still hasn't lost.

In such cases, you must immediately change your way of thinking; you need to crush his will to fight and see that he accepts defeat in his heart of hearts.

This is called knocking the bottom out. This is done by means of your *tachi*, by means of your body, and by means of your heart. There is no one way to do it.

If the enemy has completely collapsed, there is no longer a need to remain wary. If that is not the case, you must keep alert. Your enemy is also remaining alert, refusing to utterly collapse.

Whether in a battlefield fight or a one-on-one, you must keep in mind the notion of knocking the bottom out and train hard.

Renewing Yourself

This refers to a situation where, in the midst of a fight, conditions become involved, there is no room for movement, and you have to abandon your previous way of thinking and adopt a new rhythm, as if starting all over again, and then go for the win.

You renew yourself when the fighting becomes indecisive. At this point, you must change your way of thinking and go for the win using entirely different methods.

In large-scale battles as well, it is important to keep in mind the notion of renewing yourself. Given the principles of the Way of strategy, this is only natural. Look carefully into this.

Mouse's Head and Horse's Neck

This refers to a moment in battle when both sides are taken up with small matters, and conditions have become hopelessly entangled. At this point, in keeping with the strategy of "mouse's head and horse's neck," you change from a small way of thinking to a big one and transform the conditions of the fight. This is one of the tactics available to you in the Way of strategy.

It is essential that samurai embrace both ways of thinking in their daily lives, the large and the small, mouse's head and horse's neck. Whether in large-scale battle or in one-on-one combat, this should not be forgotten. Look into this very carefully.

The Commander Knows His Troops

In any type of engagement, when things are going your way, you should continually put into practice the principle of the commander knowing his troops. Using the intellectual resources of the Way of strategy, you should think of your opponents as being your own troops, be ready to make them do as you wish, and lead them around by the nose. This is the meaning of the commander knowing his troops.

You are the commander, the enemy are your troops. Adapt and invent.

Letting Go of the Hilt

Letting go of the hilt has various meanings. It can

mean to win without recourse to the sword. Or it can mean to lose *with* recourse to the sword. It is a complicated matter and cannot be discussed here. Training is important.

A Body of Rock

This means that once you have mastered the Way of strategy in body and mind, you will immediately become like a huge rock, uncuttable and unmovable. This teaching is transmitted orally.

In the above notes, I have recorded only those points that are continually on my mind concerning the practice of the sword in the *Ni Ten Ichi Ryū* school.

Since this is the first time I have written about the strengths of my school, the writing is disorganized and I have been unable to cover more detailed matters.

Even so, it should serve as a reference for those studying our school's Way of strategy.

Since my youth I have devoted myself to the Way of strategy, gained an overall knowledge of the art of the sword, disciplined myself by training the hand and the body, and have undertaken various kinds of disciplines. I have also visited other schools. Some of them were all talk; others were obsessed with clever tricks and put on a good show, but had nothing of substance to offer.

Needless to say, should you attempt to learn from these schools, hoping to discipline your body and sharpen your mind, such flashy swordsmanship will only prove a misfortune from the viewpoint of the Way of strategy. The true Way would fall into decay and be sapped of its strength.

The true Way of strategy is to win in battle, and this will remain true until hell freezes over. If you master the resources available in our Way of strategy and put them into practice, there is not the slightest doubt that you will win.

> Twelfth day, fifth month,
> Shōhō 2 (1645)
> TO: Lord Terao Magonojō
> FROM: Shinmen Musashi

> Fifth day, second month,
> Kanbun 7 (1667)
> TO: Lord Yamamoto Gensuke
> FROM: Terao Yumeyo Katsunobu

The Book of Wind

The Book of Wind　風の巻

　宮本武蔵が他の剣術流派の批評を通じて、自らの流派「二天一流」の考え方を説いた巻。固定観念に縛られず、臨機応変に戦うことを重視する。長太刀や短太刀、力任せや早さなどにこだわる流派を否定する。

【主な難しい用語や表現】

ページ

92	deviate	逸脱する, 道を踏み外す
98	convention	慣習, しきたり
91	inner secret	奥義
	make a living	生計を立てる
92	failing	欠点, 弱点
93	encompass	～を包含する
94	averse	嫌って
	overexert	(精を)出し過ぎる
96	predisposed	傾向がある
97	detest	ひどく嫌う, 憎む
	delusion	誤った考え
98	pivot	～を回転させる
	precedent	前例, 先例
101	locale	現場, 場所
102	stamping	踏みしめる
103	marsh	沼
	bog	湿地
	erratic	一貫性のない
104	novice	初心者, 見習い
	keep up with	～に遅れずについていく
107	take into consideration	～を考慮に入れる

In the Way of strategy, it is essential to know the paths followed by other schools of the Way. Here I will take up these other schools, calling this the Book of Wind.

Without knowing the paths of other schools, you cannot fully understand the Way as taught by our *Ni Ten Ichi Ryū* school. Among the other schools, there are some that use a long *tachi* and emphasize its power, making that the chief merit of their school. There are others that use a short *tachi*, called a *kodachi*, in their pursuit of the Way of strategy. And there are still others that invent a variety of *tachi* techniques and teach everything from stances with the *tachi*, fundamental forms, and inner secrets.

In this book, we will make it clear that none of these is the true Way and will reveal what is right and wrong about each of them.

The way of the sword as practiced by *Ni Ten Ichi Ryū* is different from all these schools.

Other schools use martial arts as a means of making a living. By trying to sell their product through showy displays, they have deviated from the true Way of strategy.

Some see the Way of strategy as being nothing more than swordsmanship and practice swinging the sword, learning the movements of the body, and practicing the techniques, hoping to open the path to victory. This is not the truth path, either.

Now, one at a time, I will describe the failings of the other schools.

Examine them carefully and note the differences from the principles of the *Ni Ten Ichi Ryū* school.

Other Schools' Emphasis on the Long *Tachi*

There are some schools that favor the long *tachi*.

From the perspective of my school, these schools are for the weak.

They don't seem to understand that the goal is to win, whatever the circumstances. They take the length of the *tachi* as a good in itself, and think that they will fight from a distance where the enemy's sword cannot reach them, which is why they favor the lengthy *tachi*.

There are even some who say that fighters with long arms have an advantage, even if it is only a couple of centimeters. This is the type of thing said by people ignorant of the Way of strategy.

In short, to ignorantly try to win with a long *tachi* wielded from a distance is a sign of mental weakness, of a weak Way of strategy.

When fighting at close quarters, you can't wield a long *tachi*, and you can't use it freely; it becomes a hindrance, and you end up being inferior to someone fighting with a short *wakizashi*.

Those carrying long *tachi* may have their reasons, but those reasons are nothing more than personal ones. Looked at from the right Way, this reasoning doesn't make sense. In any case, if you don't have a long *tachi* and can only use a short one, does that mean that you will necessarily lose? If you are fighting in a space that is confined both above and below, and to right and left, or where you can only use your *wakizashi*, it would go against the principles of the Way of strategy to favor the long *tachi*.

Some people aren't strong enough to use a long *tachi*. From the past it has been said, "The large encompasses the small." It is not that I have an irrational dislike for the long *tachi*. What I dislike is the persistent clinging to it.

In large-scale battles, you might compare the long *tachi* to a large number of troops and the short *tachi* to a small number. Has a small number never defeated a large number? There are many cases in which smaller numbers have beaten larger.

In the *Ni Ten Ichi Ryū* school, we are averse to giving the long *tachi* special preference. Understand this well.

Other Schools' Use of Powerful *Tachi*

There is no such thing as a powerful *tachi* or a weak *tachi*.

A *tachi* that is swung powerfully will be inaccurate and wild. And wildness by itself is not enough to win in combat.

Furthermore, if you try to cut someone with a powerful *tachi* and overexert yourself in your swing, you will find that the cutting doesn't go well. Even in test cuttings, you shouldn't try to cut powerfully.

When exchanging cuts with an enemy, no matter who he may be, you don't think of cutting weakly or cutting strongly. Or when you are trying to kill the enemy, you don't think whether you should swing powerfully or weakly. You think only of what you can do to see that the enemy dies.

If you slap the enemy's sword with too much

force, you will find that your momentum throws you off balance, invariably leading to bad results. If you hit the enemy's sword with great force, you may break your own *tachi*. That's why a powerful *tachi* is not a good one.

In large-scale engagements, if you have strong forces and try to win the battle by pushing forward with power, the enemy will push back powerfully with his own strong forces. Both forces do the same thing.

In order to win, you must be rational.

In our school, we don't think of doing the irrational, but we go for the win in any way possible by using the rational resources of the Way of strategy. Adapt and invent well.

Other School's Usage of the Short *Tachi*

It would be a mistake to think that you can win with only a short *tachi*.

In the past, swords were differentiated by their length as being long *tachi* or short *katana*.

In general, strong men can easily wield a long *tachi*. In such cases, they don't favor the short *tachi*, but prefer long weapons, such as the spear or halberd.

To think that you can use a short *tachi* to cut the enemy by taking advantage of gaps in his swings, or by leaping in to grab him, is the thinking of a predisposed mind and not good.

Besides, aiming for gaps seems all-too defensive and leads to becoming entangled, and therefore is not good. Or you could try to close with the enemy and win the day, but this doesn't work when faced with a really strong opponent.

Even for those who insist on using the short sword, and who hope to slash and drive off the enemy by spinning and leaping freely about, all of this becomes defensive, leading to entanglement, and is not a reliable way of fighting.

If this is the case, it is more to your advantage to get the certain win by holding your body straight, pursuing the enemy, and making him leap about until thoroughly confused.

The same applies to large-scale engagements. It is one of the fundamentals of the Way of strategy to abruptly drive back the enemy with a large force and destroy him on the spot.

When studying the Way of strategy out in the world, you may devote yourself daily to learning such things as parrying, dodging, disengaging, and evasion, but you might be paying too much attention to these finer points and being led astray.

The Way of strategy is a straight true path, and you must pursue the enemy and make him conform to your thoughts according to the rational principals of the Way. Learn this well.

The Numerous Sword Techniques of Other Schools

To boast of numerous sword techniques, and to teach them to students, is to make the martial arts a commercial product, a way of persuading beginners that you possess knowledge of a great many techniques. This is something that the Way of strategy detests.

In the first place, it is a delusion to think that there are many ways of cutting a person. It is not that a special path exists. Whether you know the Way of strategy or not, whether you are a woman or a child, there is not much more to it than striking, slapping, and cutting. Other than that, stabbing and slashing horizontally complete the list. If you accept the Way of strategy as the way of cutting, the finer details should not be that many.

And yet, according to place and time, when the

space above and on the sides is confined, and you are prevented from using the *tachi*, there are five ways available for holding the *tachi*. In addition, there are other ways of cutting your opponent—such as pivoting your wrists, twisting your body, jumping, and pulling back—but none of these is part of the true Way.

Pivoting, twisting, jumping, and pulling back are absolutely useless in cutting a person.

In our Way of strategy, you should hold your body and heart straight and make your opponent twist and contort, force his heart to become distorted and fall into confusion, thus seizing the moment of victory. Examine this well.

The Importance of Taking a Stance

It is wrong to emphasize the stance.

In general, the stance assumes there is no opponent, and its finer points depend on past precedent and modern convention, but in fact the establishment of such rules should not be a part of the Way as a means of combat. In battle, the primary point is to proceed in such a way as to put your opponent at a disadvantage.

As a general rule, to take up a stance is to construct an immovable position. It may mean to build a fortress or to take up a fixed stance. In any case, it means that if attacked, you have no intention of being moved. This is the everyday meaning.

However, in combat according to the Way of strategy, you should be constantly thinking of taking the initiative, whereas to take up a stance means you are waiting for the initiative. Adapt and invent well.

In combat according to the Way of strategy, the way to victory is through moving your opponent's position, by catching him by surprise, or by bewildering, frustrating, and threatening him—that is, throwing him into confusion and taking advantage of his bad timing to seize victory. If this is indeed the strategy of the Way, then taking a stance as a defensive measure is incompatible with its thinking.

In our Way of strategy, our principle is the stance of no stance, which means to take a stance but not a rigid stance.

When commencing a large-scale engagement, the cardinal rule is to know the enemy's numbers, the conditions of the battlefield, and the state of the enemy's troops, and then to position your own troops. Taking the initiative in contrast to not taking the initiative doubles your chances of victory.

If you take a defensive stance with your *tachi*, you may be able to block and beat back the enemy's swords. But this would be equivalent to taking up and wielding the spears and halberds forming the barriers that the enemy has just crossed. To attack the enemy and take the initiative, you should take up your spears and halberds from the beginning. Understand this well.

The Use of the Eyes in Other Schools

The question of where to fix the eyes varies according to the school. Some say you should fix your eyes on your opponent's *tachi*; others say the hands; still others say the face; and there are some that say it should be the feet or other parts of the body.

But whichever it is, fixing your eyes in this way will end up leading you astray and be the ruin of the Way of strategy.

For example, if you are playing foot ball, you don't need to have your eyes fixed on the ball to be able to kick it while going through various complicated movements, or to kick it while spinning around. You become accustomed to it, so there is no need to have your eyes firmly fixed.

Likewise when watching acrobats, since they are familiar with their trade, they can balance a door on their nose while juggling a number of swords. They are not fixing their eyes on anything, but because they have grown accustomed to it, they have learned to do it as a matter of course.

The same applies to the Way of strategy. By engaging in combat now and then, you learn to judge the quality of your opponents' hearts, and if you firmly follow the Way, you learn to know everything from the distance of a sword to its speed. In the Way of strategy, seeing means to see into the heart of your opponent.

In large-scale engagements, the Way of strategy calls for you to fix your eyes on the number of enemy troops and on their present condition. As to the question of the two ways of seeing, the strong and the weak, you must look strongly and see into the enemy's heart. You must see the present situation in terms of locale, keep an eye on general conditions, and watch for overall developments, and go straight for the win as you take advantage of the ups and downs of the moment.

Regardless of whether the number of combatants is large or small, you should not be distracted by smaller things.

As mentioned previously, if you turn your eyes to smaller matters and forget the big picture, you will become hesitant and surely lose the chance to win.

Examine this well and practice hard.

Footwork in Other Schools

There are various ways of moving the feet quickly, such as the floating foot, leaping foot, hopping foot, stamping foot, and running foot.

However, looked at from the perspective of our Way of strategy, none of these really does the trick.

The reason we do not like the floating foot is that, in battle, the feet will float in any case, and rather than floating, you need to keep your feet firmly planted on the ground.

The reason for not liking the leaping foot is that the act itself is distracting to your mind and restricts whatever action you might take next. It is not as though you are going to do a lot of leaping anyway, so we do not recommend it.

We do not like the hopping foot because if you are conscious of the action itself, it will not go smoothly.

The stamping foot is particularly bad because the

feet are in a defensive, waiting stance.

There are many other ways of achieving fast footwork, such as the running foot, but since you may have to fight in places like marshes, bogs, mountain streams, rocky areas, and narrow roads, there are times when fancy, speedy footwork is just not possible.

In our Way of strategy, the feet are moved as in ordinary walking It is as if you are walking down the road in front of you, just as you would usually do. Matching your movements to your opponent's, whether moving quickly or moving quietly, you keep in tune with the state of your body. Without overdoing it or underdoing it, you take care that your footwork does not become erratic.

In large-scale engagements as well, footwork is important. This doesn't mean that, with no knowledge of the enemy's intentions, you attack with such erratic speed that something goes wrong with your rhythm, making it difficult to win.

On the other hand, if you move quietly, you may miss the chance to swiftly claim victory when the enemy starts to collapse.

It is essential that you catch the moment that the enemy becomes disordered and push him relentlessly, thereby gaining the win. Train hard.

The Emphasis in Other Schools on Fast Swordplay

It is wrong, as other schools do, to advocate speedy swordplay.

Whether you can call swordplay fast or slow depends on whether its timing is too early or too late.

To a master in the Way of strategy, such swordplay does not in itself appear to be fast.

For example, a fast runner can cover between 160 and 200 kilometers a day, and he is not even running from morning to night. But a novice can run all day long and still not be as effective.

In Noh drama, when a good performer sings with a poor performer, the latter falls behind and becomes nervous. The drums in the Noh play *Oimatsu* have a slow rhythm, but poor performers have trouble keeping up with it. In the play *Takasago*, the music contains a sense of urgency, but it should not be played fast.

If you move swiftly, you may fall and lose your timing, but that does not mean that slowness is good. The movement of a master of his art seems to be leisurely, but in fact it is perfectly timed. In whatever field you choose, those familiar with that field never look rushed. Learn the principles of the Way through these examples.

In the Way of strategy, speed is not considered a good in itself. In fact, in places like marshes and bogs, neither your body nor your feet can move quickly. And neither can you cut quickly with your *tachi*.

Even should you try to cut quickly, it won't be as fast as if you were using a fan or a short sword, and if you try some clever trick, this is not likely to work either. Understand the differences well.

In large-scale engagements, you should not feel hurried or rushed. If you keep in mind the notion of "holding down the pillow"—that is, nipping the enemy's action in the bud—you will never be late.

And if the enemy rushes into action without any reason, you should turn your back on it, so to speak, and respond quietly, not being dragged into action by your opponent.

Adapt this and practice hard.

The Depths and the Surface in Other Schools

In the Way of strategy, where is the surface and

where are the depths?

In some arts, the mysteries and hidden secrets of the art are sometimes spoken of, and they seem to possess hidden depths. But in the rationale of fighting, there is no such thing as fighting on the surface and cutting with the depths.

In my school of the Way, we teach beginners what they can pick up easily according to their ability. What can be understood easily is taught first, and what is difficult to grasp is taught later.

However, since most learn how to fight using a sword, there is no such thing as an entryway into the depths.

After all, the world speaks of going into the depths of a mountain, and if you go far enough, you reach the exit. In all arts, there are times when you come in contact with the depths, and there are times when using the surface is fine.

In the Way of strategy taught here, there is no thought of deciding what to hide and what to reveal. For that reason, we prefer not to make use of pledges and punishments in transmitting the way of our school.

According to the ability of the learner of our Way, we teach him the true path, correct bad habits picked up while learning the Way, see him eventually enter the true path of the authentic warrior, and develop in him an unwavering heart. This is the teaching of our Way of strategy. Train hard.

Above, in the Book of Wind, I have outlined in nine articles the Way of strategy of other schools.

I could have given more detail about the surface and depths of each school, but I chose not to describe which technique belongs to which school.

The reason for this is that each school has its own viewpoint, and their way of thinking depends on the individual and conditions, so that there are subtle differences in their view of matters.

Taking the future into consideration, I didn't include the path of the *tachi* and other matters, but simply divided up the main characteristics of other schools into nine categories.

Looking at things from the way of the world and from common human reasoning, we can see that these schools have certain predispositions—some favoring the long *tachi*, others touting the short, some paying particular attention to strength or weakness when striking, and still others emphasizing roughness or fineness. Even without describing the surface and depths of these schools, everything should be clear to you by now.

In my *Ni Ten Ichi Ryū* school, the *tachi* has no

surface or depths. There are no secret teachings to the stance. Simply have the right mentality and understand the merits of the Way. This is the most important thing in our school.

> Twelfth day, fifth month,
> Shōhō 2 (1645)
> TO: Lord Terao Magonojō
> FROM: Shinmen Musashi

> Fifth day, second month,
> Kanbun 7 (1667)
> TO: Lord Yamamoto Gensuke
> FROM: Terao Yumeyo Katsunobu

The Book of
Emptiness

The Book of Emptiness　空の巻

　宮本武蔵が兵法の修行から到達した境地「空」について書いた巻。空とは何もないことだが、あることを知ってはじめてないことを知ることができる。心に曇りや迷いがなく、智・利・道を備えることで、その心は空の域に達する。

【主な難しい用語や表現】

ページ
111	negligent	怠慢な, 不注意な
112	haze	かすみ, もや
	distortion	歪曲
	bias	偏見, 先入見

In describing the *Nitō Ichi Ryū* school in the Book of Emptiness, "emptiness" refers to something without shape, to something whose shape you cannot know.

By knowing the rationale and shape of a thing, you first realize when it has none. This is emptiness.

Some people in the world have the bad habit of calling something empty when they cannot understand it, but this is not true emptiness. It is nothing but a delusion of the mind.

Concerning the Way of strategy and the path of a samurai, those who don't know the way of the warrior may think it empty, but it is not. There are those who have many delusions and are unsure of their way and call it emptiness, but this is not true emptiness either.

Samurai must first learn the path of strategy, acquire the martial arts, understand how to walk the path of a warrior, have no delusions in their hearts, never be negligent, polish both their hearts and minds, and hone their skills in seeing both the large and the small. It is here in this clear space of the heart, without the least bit of haze or cloud of doubt, that we find true emptiness.

Before you know the true Way, you might think that you are traveling a sure path, whether relying on Buddhism or the conventions of the world. You may think that is a good thing, but judged by the standards of the world and by the true Way, there is distortion and bias in your mind, and you have deviated from the true Way.

You must understand the reason for this, maintain a straight position, take your original heart as the Way, carry out the Way of strategy broadly, do it correctly and clearly, grasp the big picture, make emptiness your Way, and see the Way as emptiness.

In emptiness, there is good but no evil. If you take knowledge as the basis of reason and follow the Way of strategy, what is left is a state of emptiness in which everything has been erased.

> Twelfth day, fifth month,
> Shōhō 2 (1645)
> TO: Lord Terao Magonojō
> FROM: Shinmen Musashi
>
> Fifth day, second month,
> Kanbun 7 (1667)

TO: Lord Yamamoto Gensuke
FROM: Terao Yumeyo Katsunobu

Word List

A

- [ ] **abandon** 動 ①捨てる、放棄する ②（計画などを）中止する、断念する
- [ ] **ability** 名 ①できること、（～する）能力 ②才能
- [ ] **about** 熟 be about to まさに～しようとしている、～するところだ be unconcerned about ～に無関心である bring about 引き起こす
- [ ] **above** 熟 above all else とりわけ、何にもまして from straight above 真上から
- [ ] **abrupt** 形 ①突然の、不意の ②（坂などが）急な
- [ ] **abruptly** 副 不意に、突然、急に
- [ ] **absolutely** 副 完全に、確実に
- [ ] **absorbed** 形 すっかり心を奪われた、夢中の
- [ ] **accept** 動 ①受け入れる ②同意する、認める
- [ ] **accompany** 動 ①ついていく、つきそう ②（～に）ともなって起こる
- [ ] **accompanying** 形 付随の
- [ ] **accomplished** 形 ①完成した ②（技量に）優れた、熟達した
- [ ] **accordance** 名 一致、適合 in accordance with ～に従って

- [ ] **according to** ～に従って、～によれば［よると］
- [ ] **accordingly** 副 ①それに応じて、適宜に ②従って、（～と）いうわけだから
- [ ] **accustom** 動《– to ～》～に慣れさせる
- [ ] **accustomed** 熟 become accustomed to ～に慣れる get accustomed to ～に慣れる
- [ ] **achieve** 動 成し遂げる、達成する、成功を収める
- [ ] **achieved** 形 （努力の結果として）達成［獲得］された
- [ ] **acquaint** 動 （～を）熟知させる、知り合いにさせる
- [ ] **acquainted** 熟 be well acquainted with ～によく通じている
- [ ] **acquire** 動 ①（努力して）獲得する、確保する ②（学力、技術などを）習得する
- [ ] **acquisition** 名 取得、獲得
- [ ] **acrobat** 名 曲芸師
- [ ] **act** 名 行為、行い
- [ ] **activity** 名 活動、活気
- [ ] **actor** 名 俳優、役者

114

Word List

□ **actual** 形 実際の, 現実の

□ **actually** 副 実際に, 本当に, 実は

□ **adapt** 動 適応する［させる］adapt to ～に適合する

□ **adaptation** 名 順応, 適応

□ **addition** 名 付加, 追加, 添加 in addition 加えて, さらに

□ **adhere** 動 (～に) くっつく adhere to ～を忠実に守る

□ **adherent** 名 追随者, 支持者, 信奉者

□ **adhesive** 形 粘着性の, すぐにくっつく

□ **adjust** 動 ①適応する［させる］, 慣れる ②調整する

□ **adjustment** 名 ①調整, 調節 ②適応

□ **admirable** 形 賞賛に値する, 見事な

□ **adopt** 動 採択する, 選ぶ

□ **advance** 名 進歩, 前進

□ **advantage** 名 有利な点［立場］, 強み, 優越 take advantage of ～を利用する, ～につけ込む

□ **advantageous** 形 都合のよい, 有利な

□ **advocate** 動 主張する, 提唱する

□ **adze** 名 (木工用の) 手おの

□ **aesthete** 名 審美眼のある人

□ **afford** 動 《can ～》～することができる, ～する (経済的・時間的な) 余裕がある

□ **after all** やはり, 結局

□ **against** 熟 come up against ～に直面する, (障害・困難・問題・反対など) に出くわす push against ～を押す

□ **age** 熟 at the age of ～歳のときに

□ **aim** 動 ①(武器などを) 向ける ②ねらう, 目指す

□ **Akiyama** 名 秋山《人名》

□ **alarm** 動 ①はっとさせる ②警報を発する

□ **alcove** 名 アルコーブ《部屋の一部引っ込んだところ》 decorative alcove 床の間

□ **alert** 形 油断のない, 用心深い, 機敏な keep alert 警戒を怠らない 名 警報, 警戒

□ **all** 熟 above all else とりわけ, 何にもまして after all やはり, 結局 all at once いっせいに, 突然, 出し抜けに all day long 一日中, 終日 all over ～中で, 全体に亘って, ～での至る所で, 全て終わって, もうだめで in all of which それら全ての中で not good at all お話にならない not ～ at all 少しも［全然］～ない

□ **all-important** 形 極めて重要な

□ **all-out attack** 総攻撃

□ **all-too** 副 あまりにも～すぎる.

□ **allow** 動 ①許す, 《– … to ～》…が～するのを可能にする, …に～させておく ②与える

□ **also** 熟 not only ～ but also … ～だけでなく…もまた

□ **alternatively** 副 二者択一として, その代わりとして

□ **altogether** 副 まったく, 全然, 全部で

□ **amiss** 副 間違って go amiss (物事が) 順調にいかない

□ **analogy** 名 ①類似 (点) ②類推

□ **anger** 動 怒る, ～を怒らせる

□ **announce** 動 (人に) 知らせる, 公表する

□ **another** 熟 at one time or another (正確な日付は覚えていないが) いつだったか

□ **anticipate** 動 ①予期する ②先んじる

□ **any** 熟 in any case とにかく in any way 決して, 多少なりとも

□ **anyone** 代 ①《疑問文・条件節で》

115

The Book of Five Rings

誰か ②《否定文で》誰も（〜ない）③
《肯定文で》誰でも

□ **anyway** 副 ①いずれにせよ，とも
かく ②どんな方法でも

□ **apart** 副 ばらばらに，離れて **come
apart** バラバラになる，壊れる **move
apart** 離れていく

□ **apparently** 副 見たところ〜らし
い，明らかに

□ **appear** 動 ①現れる，見えてく
る ②（〜のように）見える，〜らしい
appear to するように見える

□ **appearance** 名 外見，印象

□ **applicable** 形 適用できる，応用で
きる

□ **apply** 動 ①あてはまる ②適用する
apply pressure 圧力をかける

□ **appreciate** 動 ①正しく評価する，
よさがわかる ②ありがたく思う

□ **approach** 名 接近，（〜へ）近づく
道

□ **arch** 動 アーチ状にする **arch back**
背中を反らす

□ **archer** 名 射手，弓の射手

□ **archery** 名 弓矢，弓術

□ **Arima Kihei** 有馬喜兵衛《人名》

□ **around** 熟 **be led around by
the nose**（人）に翻弄される **lead
someone around by the nose**（人）
を思うままに操る **look around** ま
わりを見回す

□ **arrive at** 〜に着く

□ **arrow** 名 矢，矢のようなもの

□ **art** 名 技，術 **art of** 〜術 **art of
strategy** 戦略の技術，兵法 **martial
arts** 武芸

□ **article** 名 箇条，項目

□ **artisan** 名 伝統工芸などの職人，熟
練工

□ **artist** 名 芸術家

□ **artistic** 形 芸術的な，芸術（家）の

□ **as** 熟 **as a matter of course** 当然

のことながら **as best one can** 精一
杯，できるだけ **as far as** 〜と同じ
くらい遠く，〜まで，〜に関する限りは
as for 〜に関しては，〜はどうかと言
うと **as if** あたかも〜のように，まる
で〜みたいに **as long as** 〜する以上
は，〜である限りは **as soon as** 〜す
るとすぐ，〜するや否や **as though**
あたかも〜のように，まるで〜みたい
に **as to** 〜に関しては，〜については，
〜に応じて なお，その上，同
様に **as well as** 〜と同様に **as you
wish** 望み通りに **as 〜 as one can**
できる限り〜 **as 〜 as possible** で
きるだけ〜 **be known as** 〜として
知られている **just as**（ちょうど）で
あろうとおり **pass oneself off as**
自分が〜になりすます **see 〜 as …**
〜を…と考える **such as** たとえば〜，
〜のような **such 〜 as …** …のよう
な〜 **the same 〜 as …** …と同じ
（ような）〜

□ **aside** 副 わきへ（に），離れて

□ **aspect** 名 ①状況，局面，側面 ②外
観，様子

□ **aspire** 動 熱望する，切望する
aspire to 〜を希望する

□ **assemble** 動 ①集める，集まる
②組み立てる

□ **assume** 動 ①仮定する，当然のこ
とと思う ②引き受ける

□ **assure** 動 ①保障する，請け負う
②確信をもって言う

□ **assured** 形 確信して

□ **astray** 副 迷って，正しい道からそ
れて **be led astray** 惑わされる **lead
someone astray**（人）を道に迷わせ
る

□ **at** 熟 **at a time** 一度に，続けざまに
at close quarters 間近に，接近して
at ease ゆとりがあって **at first** 最
初は，初めのうちは **at hand** 近くに，
目前に，すぐ使えるように **at large**
全体として，広く **at once** すぐに，同
時に **at one time or another**（正確
な日付は覚えていないが）いつだった
か **at one's disposal**（人が）自由に

116

できる[使える], 意のままに使える
at that moment その時に, その瞬間に **at the age of ~** 歳のときに **at the moment** 今は **at the time of ~**の時[際]に **at this point** 現在のところ **at times** 時には

- [ ] **attached** 動 attach（取りつける）の過去, 過去分詞 形ついている, 結びついた, 《be – to ~》~に未練[愛着]がある

- [ ] **attack** 動 襲う, 攻める **attack head-on** 正面から攻撃する 名攻撃 **all-out attack** 総攻撃 **single-timing attack** 一拍子（ひとつびょうし）打ち

- [ ] **attacker** 名攻撃者, 敵

- [ ] **attain** 動達成する, 成し遂げる, 達する

- [ ] **attempt** 動試みる, 企てる **attempt to ~**しようと試みる 名試み, 企て, 努力

- [ ] **attempting** 熟 **in attempting to ~**しようとして

- [ ] **attention** 名①注意, 集中 ②配慮, 手当て, 世話 **pay attention to ~**に注意を払う

- [ ] **attitude** 名姿勢, 態度, 心構え **take the attitude** その態度を取る

- [ ] **authentic** 形本物の, 信頼のおける, 確実な

- [ ] **available** 形利用[使用・入手]できる, 得られる

- [ ] **averse** 形嫌って

- [ ] **avoid** 動避ける, (~を)しないようにする

- [ ] **aware** 形①気がついて, 知って ②(~の)認識のある **be aware of ~**に気がついている

- [ ] **awesomeness** 名威厳性, すばらしさ

- [ ] **awkward** 形①不器用な, 不格好な ②やっかいな, やりにくい

B

- [ ] **back** 熟 **arch back** 背中を反らす **bring back** 戻す, 呼び戻す, 持ち帰る **drive back**（敵などを）追い返す **force them back** 力ずくで無理やり戻す **hold back**（事実・本心などを）隠す,（感情を）抑える, 自制する **push back** 押し返す, 押しのける **put back**（もとの場所に）戻す, 返す **shrink back** 身体を縮める **turn one's back on ~**に背を向ける, ~を無視する

- [ ] **badly** 副①悪く, まずく, へたに ②とても, ひどく

- [ ] **balance** 名①均衡, 平均, 落ち着き ②てんびん ③残高, 差額 **catch someone off balance**（人）の意表を突く **throw ~ off balance ~**の平衡[均衡]を失わせる 動釣り合いをとる

- [ ] **balanced** 形均衡を保っている

- [ ] **bamboo** 形竹の

- [ ] **barricaded** 形バリケードで塞いだ

- [ ] **barrier** 名さく, 防壁, 障害(物), 障壁

- [ ] **base** 動《 – on ~》~に基礎を置く, 基づく

- [ ] **basic** 名《-s》基礎, 基本, 必需品

- [ ] **basis** 名①土台, 基礎 ②基準, 原理 ③根拠

- [ ] **battle** 名戦闘, 戦い

- [ ] **battlefield** 名戦場

- [ ] **beam** 名長い角材, 梁 **floor beam** 床梁 **grooved beam** 鴨居

- [ ] **bear** 動①運ぶ ②支える ③耐える **be brought to bear** 用に供させる **bear down on ~**を威圧する

- [ ] **beat** 動打つ

- [ ] **beaten** 動 beat（打つ）の過去分詞

- [ ] **because of ~**のために, ~の理由で

- [ ] **become** 熟 **become accustomed**

to ～に慣れる **become disordered** 障害される **become distorted** ゆがむ **become entangled** もつれる，絡まる **become fixated on** ～に執着している **become flustered** うろたえる

- [ ] **before-after shout** 先後の声
- [ ] **befuddle** 動 (人) を混乱させる
- [ ] **beginner** 名 初心者
- [ ] **beginning** 名 初め，始まり
- [ ] **behind** 前①～の後ろに，～の背後に ②～に遅れて，～に劣って 副①後ろに，背後に ②遅れて，劣って **be left behind** 置いていかれる **fall behind** 取り残される，後れを取る **leave behind** あとにする，～を置き去りにする
- [ ] **being** 動 be (～である) の現在分詞 名 存在，生命，人間 **one's being** 自分の存在
- [ ] **belatedly** 副 遅れて
- [ ] **belly** 名 腹
- [ ] **belong** 動《– to ～》～に属する，～のものである
- [ ] **below** 副 下に [へ]
- [ ] **beneath** 前 ～の下に [の]，～より低い
- [ ] **benefit** 名 利益，恩恵
- [ ] **bent** 形 曲がった
- [ ] **besides** 前①～に加えて，～のほかに ②《否定文・疑問文で》～を除いて 副 その上，さらに
- [ ] **best** as best one can 精一杯，できるだけ
- [ ] **bewilder** 動 当惑させる，まごつかせる
- [ ] **beyond** 前 ～を越えて，～の向こうに
- [ ] **bias** 名 偏見，先入見，バイアス
- [ ] **big** 熟 take a big picture 全体像を捉える
- [ ] **bit** 名 小片，少量

- [ ] **blade** 名 (刀・ナイフなどの) 刃
- [ ] **blinding speed** 目にも止まらぬ速さ
- [ ] **blink** 動 まばたき (を) する
- [ ] **blow** 名 打撃
- [ ] **board** 名 板 cutting board まな板
- [ ] **boast** 動 自慢する，誇る，鼻にかける
- [ ] **bodily** 形 身体上の，体の 副 身体的に
- [ ] **bog** 名 湿地
- [ ] **bookshelf** 名 本棚
- [ ] **bookshelves** 名 bookshelf (本棚) の複数
- [ ] **both A and B** AもBも
- [ ] **bottom** 名 底，下部，根底 knock the bottom out 根底から覆す
- [ ] **bout** 名 一勝負
- [ ] **bow** 名 弓，弓状のもの
- [ ] **brief** 名 要点，概要 in brief 手短に
- [ ] **bring about** 引き起こす
- [ ] **bring back** 戻す，呼び戻す，持ち帰る
- [ ] **bring down** 打ち降ろす，仕留める
- [ ] **bring out** (物) をとりだす，引き出す
- [ ] **broad** 形 幅の広い broader perspective 大局的見地
- [ ] **broadly** 副 大ざっぱに，露骨に
- [ ] **broken down into**《be –》～に分解される
- [ ] **brought to bear**《be –》用に供させる
- [ ] **bud** 名 芽，つぼみ nip ～ in the bud ～の芽を摘む，未然に防ぐ
- [ ] **Buddha** 名 仏陀，釈迦《仏教の開祖》
- [ ] **Buddhism** 名 仏教，仏道，仏法
- [ ] **Buddhist** 形 仏教 (徒) の，仏陀の 名 仏教徒

- [ ] **bullet** 名銃弾, 弾丸状のもの
- [ ] **burglar** 名 (夜間に侵入する) 泥棒
- [ ] **burst** 動①爆発する [させる] ②破裂する [させる] **burst out with** (感情を) 急に表す, 激発する
- [ ] **business** 熟 **in the world of business** 商売の世界では
- [ ] **but** 熟 **not only ~ but also …** ~だけでなく…もまた **not ~ but …** ~ではなくて… **nothing but** ただ~だけ, ~にすぎない, ~のほかは何も…ない
- [ ] **buttock** 名《通例-s》尻
- [ ] **by** 熟 **by and large** 概して **by means of** ~を用いて, ~によって **by now** 今のところ, 今ごろまでには **by oneself** 一人で, 自分だけで, 独力で

C

- [ ] **call for** ~を求める, 訴える, ~を呼び求める, 呼び出す
- [ ] **calm** 形穏やかな, 落ち着いた **calm and collected** 静かに落ち着いた **remain calm** 冷静さを保つ
- [ ] **calmly** 副落ち着いて, 静かに
- [ ] **calmness** 名静けさ
- [ ] **can** 熟 **as best one can** 精一杯, できるだけ **as ~ as one can** できる限り~
- [ ] **capability** 名能力, 才能
- [ ] **capable** 形①《be – of ~ [~ing]》~の能力 [資質] がある ②有能な
- [ ] **captain** 名船長
- [ ] **cardinal** 形主要な **cardinal rule** 鉄則
- [ ] **care** 熟 **care for** ~の世話をする, ~を扱う, ~が好きである, ~を大事に思う **take care** 気をつける, 注意する **take care to** よく (注意して) [入念に] ~する

- [ ] **carpenter** 名大工
- [ ] **carpentry** 名大工仕事
- [ ] **carry on** ①続ける ②持ち運ぶ
- [ ] **carry out** 実行 [遂行] する
- [ ] **case** 熟 **in any case** とにかく **in the case of** ~の場合は
- [ ] **catch someone off balance** (人) の意表を突く
- [ ] **category** 名カテゴリー, 種類, 部類
- [ ] **cautious** 形用心深い, 慎重な
- [ ] **ceiling** 名天井
- [ ] **centimeter** 名センチメートル《長さの単位》
- [ ] **ceremony** 名①儀式, 式典 ②礼儀, 作法 **tea ceremony** 茶道
- [ ] **certain** 形①確実な, 必ず~する ②(人が) 確信した ③ある ④いくらかの
- [ ] **certainly** 副確かに, 必ず
- [ ] **challenge** 動挑む, 試す
- [ ] **chance** 形偶然の **chance to strike** ~に行き当たる
- [ ] **change** 熟 **exhibit a change** 変化を見せる
- [ ] **changeability** 名変わりやすい性質
- [ ] **character** 名①特性, 個性 ②文字, 記号
- [ ] **characteristic** 名特徴, 特性, 特色, 持ち味
- [ ] **chest** 名胸
- [ ] **chief** 形最高位の, 第一の, 主要な
- [ ] **China** 名中国《国名》
- [ ] **Chinese** 形中国 (人) の
- [ ] **chronicle** 名年代記, 記録, 物語 **war chronicle** 軍記, 戦記
- [ ] **circumstance** 名 (周囲の) 事情, 状況, 環境
- [ ] **claim** 動①主張する ②要求する, 請求する **claim victory** 勝利を収め

る

- □ **clear** 形 はっきりした, 明白な
- □ **clearly** 副 明らかに, はっきりと
- □ **clever** 形 ①頭のよい, 利口な ②器用な, 上手な
- □ **cleverly** 副 (手先などが) 器用に, 上手に
- □ **cling** 動 くっつく, しがみつく, 執着する
- □ **clinging** 形 くっつく
- □ **close** 熟 at close quarters 間近に, 接近して close the wedge くさびをしめる get in close 入り込む move in close 近寄る
- □ **clutter** 動 (心を) 取り乱す
- □ **collapse** 名 崩壊, 倒壊 動 崩壊する, 崩れる, 失敗する
- □ **collected** 形 (人が感情を抑えて) 落ち着いた, 冷静な calm and collected 静かに落ち着いた
- □ **collide** 動 ぶつかる, 衝突する collide with ~にぶつかる
- □ **collision** 名 衝突, 不一致, あつれき
- □ **combat** 名 戦闘
- □ **combatant** 名 戦闘員
- □ **come** 熟 come and go 行き交う, 去来する, 移り変わる come apart バラバラになる come down in the world 落ちぶれる come in contact with ~と接触する [触れ合う], ~に出くわす come out 出てくる, 出掛ける, 姿を現す come up against ~に直面する, (障害・困難・問題・反対など) に出くわす When it comes to ~に関して言えば
- □ **commander** 名 司令官, 指揮官
- □ **commence** 動 始める, 始まる, 開始する
- □ **comment** 名 論評, 解説, コメント
- □ **commerce** 名 商業, 貿易
- □ **commercial** 形 商業の, 営利的な

- □ **commit** 動 (~と) 約束する, (~に) 全力を傾ける commit to memory 記憶する
- □ **companion** 名 仲間, 連れ
- □ **comparable** 形 比較できる, 匹敵する
- □ **compare** 動 ①比較する, 対照する ②たとえる
- □ **compared to** 《be – 》~と比較して, ~に比べれば
- □ **compared with** 《be – 》~と比較して, ~に比べれば
- □ **complement** 名 補足 (物), 補充 full complement 全装備
- □ **complete** 形 完全な, まったくの, 完成した 動 完成させる
- □ **completely** 副 完全に, すっかり
- □ **complicated** 形 ①複雑な ②むずかしい, 困難な
- □ **composure** 名 平静, 落ち着き
- □ **comprehend** 動 ①よく理解する ②包含する
- □ **concentrate** 動 一点に集める [集まる], 集中させる [する]
- □ **concept** 名 概念, 観念, テーマ
- □ **concern** 動 ①関係する, 《be -ed in [with] ~》~に関係している ②心配する, 《be -ed about [for] ~》~を心配する 名 ①関心事 ②関心, 心配
- □ **concerning** 前 ~に関して
- □ **condition** 名 ①(健康) 状態, 境遇 ②《-s》状況, 様子 overall condition 概況
- □ **confident** 形 自信のある, 自信に満ちた
- □ **confine** 動 制限する, 閉じ込める
- □ **confined** 形 (空間・区域などが) 狭い, 非常に小さい confined space 限定空間
- □ **confirm** 動 確かめる, 確かにする
- □ **conform** 動 (規則・慣習などに)

従う, 順応する

□ **confront** 動 ①直面する, 立ち向かう ②突き合わせる, 比較する

□ **confrontation** 名 対立, 直面

□ **Confucian** 名 儒者

□ **Confucianism** 名 儒教

□ **confused** 形 困惑した, 混乱した

□ **confusion** 名 混乱 (状態)

□ **conquer** 動 征服する, 制圧する

□ **conscious** 形 (状況などを) 意識している, 自覚している conscious of ～を意識している

□ **consciously** 副 意識して, 自覚して, 故意に

□ **consider** 動 ①考慮する, ～しようと思う ②(～と) みなす ③気にかける, 思いやる

□ **considerable** 形 相当な, かなりの, 重要な

□ **consideration** 名 ①考慮, 考察 ②考慮すべきこと take ～ into consideration ～を考慮に入れる

□ **considered** 形 熟慮した [よく考えた] 上での, 考え抜かれた

□ **consist** 動 ①《– of ～》(部分・要素から) 成る ②《– in ～》～に存在する, ～にある

□ **constant** 形 絶えない, 一定の, 不変の

□ **constantly** 副 絶えず, いつも, 絶え間なく

□ **construct** 動 建設する, 組み立てる

□ **construction** 名 構造, 建設, 工事, 建物

□ **contact** 熟 come in contact with ～と接触する [触れ合う], ～に出くわす make contact 接触する physical contact 身体的接触

□ **contagious** 形 接触伝染性の, 移りやすい

□ **contain** 動 含む, 入っている

□ **container** 名 容器, 入れ物

□ **contend** 動 争う, 競う, 論争する, 強く主張する

□ **contender** 名 競争者

□ **context** 名 文脈, 前後関係, コンテクスト in that context その意味で

□ **continually** 副 継続的に, 絶えず, ひっきりなしに

□ **continuously** 副 連続して, 絶え間なく, 変わりなく

□ **contort** 動 ～をねじる

□ **contrast** 名 対照, 対比 in contrast to ～と大いに異なって

□ **control** 名 ①管理, 支配 (力) ②抑制

□ **convention** 名 慣習, しきたり

□ **copy** 動 写す, まねる

□ **corps** 名 軍団, 部隊

□ **correct** 形 正しい, 適切な, りっぱな 動 (誤りを) 訂正する, 直す

□ **correctly** 副 正しく, 正確に

□ **could have done** ～だったかもしれない《仮定法》

□ **counter** 動 反対 [対抗] する

□ **couple of** 《a–》2, 3の

□ **course** 熟 as a matter of course 当然のことながら matter of course もちろんの事, 当たり前の事 of course もちろん, 当然

□ **cover** 動 ①覆う, 包む, 隠す ②扱う, (～に) わたる, 及ぶ ③代わりを務める ④補う

□ **craftsman** 名 職人, 熟練工

□ **cramp** 動 けいれんする

□ **cramped** 形 窮屈な

□ **create** 動 創造する, 生み出す, 引き起こす

□ **crisis** 名 ①危機, 難局 ②重大局面 ride out the crisis 危機を乗り切る

□ **cross** 動 渡る

□ **crossing** 動 cross (横切る) の過

The Book of Five Rings

去, 過去分詞 图横断, 交差点, 横断歩
道, 踏み切り **make a crossing** 横断
をする

□ **crosswise** 形交差した

□ **crucial** 形①重大な, 決定的な ②
致命的な, 正念場で

□ **crush** 動押しつぶす, 砕く, 粉々に
する **crush ~ underfoot** ~を踏み
にじる

□ **cultivate** 動耕す, 栽培する, (才
能などを) 養う, 育成する

□ **cut down** 切り倒す, 打ちのめす

□ **cutting** 動 cut (切る) の現在分詞
图①切ること, 裁断, カッティング
②(新聞などの) 切り抜き, (挿し木用
の) 切り枝 **cutting board** まな板

D

□ **daily** 形毎日の, 日常の 副毎日, 日
ごとに

□ **damage** 動損害を与える, 損なう

□ **day** 熟 **all day long** 一日中, 終日
day and night 昼も夜も **It may
take ~ days to …** …するには~日
かかるだろう **one day** (過去の) ある
日, (未来の) いつか **these days**
このごろ

□ **daybreak** 图夜明け

□ **death** 图死, 死ぬこと **life or
death struggle** 死ぬか生きるかの戦
い

□ **decay** 图腐敗, 衰え

□ **decision** 图決定, 決心

□ **decline** 图下り坂, 衰え, 衰退

□ **decorative** 形装飾的な, 装飾用
の **decorative alcove** 床の間

□ **defeat** 動打ち破る, 負かす

□ **defense** 图防御, 守備

□ **defensive** 形防御の, 守備の

□ **deflect** 動そらす

□ **deftness** 图器用さ, 熟練さ

□ **deity** 图神, 神性

□ **delicate** 形①繊細な, 壊れやすい
②淡い ③敏感な, きゃしゃな

□ **deliver** 動①配達する, 伝える ②
達成する, 果たす

□ **delusion** 图誤った考え

□ **depend** 動《 – on [upon] ~》①~
を頼る, ~を当てにする ②~による

□ **deprive** 動奪う, 取り上げる
deprive ~ of … ~から…を奪う

□ **depth** 图深さ, 奥行き, 深いところ

□ **depths** 图底, 最深部

□ **describe** 動 (言葉で) 描写する, 特
色を述べる, 説明する

□ **description** 图 (言葉で) 記述 (す
ること), 描写 (すること) **general
description** 概要

□ **desire** 图欲望, 欲求, 願望

□ **desperate** 形①絶望的な, 見込み
のない ②ほしくてたまらない, 必死
の

□ **destroy** 動破壊する, 絶滅させる,
無効にする

□ **detach** 動引き離す, はずす

□ **detail** 图①細部, 《-s》詳細 ②《-s》
個人情報 **finer details** 細部 **go into
detail** 詳しく [詳細に] 述べる [説明
する]

□ **detailed** 形詳細な, 詳しい

□ **determine** 動①決心する [させ
る] ②決定する [させる]

□ **detest** 動ひどく嫌う, 憎む

□ **develop** 動①発達する [させる]
②開発する

□ **development** 图①発達, 発展
②開発

□ **deviate** 動逸脱する, 道を踏み外
す **deviate from** ~から外れる

□ **devote** 動①(~を…に) 捧げる
②《 – oneself to ~》~に専念する

□ **diagonally** 副対角線上に

122

□ **different from**《be –》〜と違う

□ **differentiate** 動①違いが出てくる ②識別する, 区別する, 差別化する

□ **differentiated** 形分化した

□ **direction** 名①方向, 方角 ②《-s》指示, 説明書 ③指導, 指揮 **in one direction** 同一の方向に

□ **directly** 副①じかに ②まっすぐに ③ちょうど

□ **disadvantage** 名不利な立場[条件], 損失

□ **disappear** 動見えなくなる, 姿を消す, なくなる

□ **disarray** 名混乱, 無秩序 (状態) **in disarray** 混乱して

□ **discern** 動見分ける, 識別する

□ **discerning** 形優れた判断力[識別力]を持つ **discerning eye** 鑑識眼

□ **discernment** 名優れた判断力

□ **discipline** 名規律, しつけ 動訓練する, しつける **discipline oneself** 自己を鍛える

□ **discuss** 動議論[検討]する

□ **discussion** 名討議, 討論

□ **disengage** 動離れる, 外れる **disengage oneself** 自由になる

□ **dislike** 動嫌う 名反感, いや気

□ **disordered** 形乱れた, 乱雑な **become disordered** 障害される

□ **disorganized** 形まとまりのない

□ **display** 名展示, 陳列, 表出

□ **disposal** 名処分, 廃棄 **at one's disposal** (人が)自由にできる[使える], 意のままに使える

□ **disposition** 名①気質, 気持ち ②配置, 配列

□ **disrupt** 動(国家・組織を)分裂させる, (交通網などを)途絶させる

□ **distance** 名距離, 隔たり, 遠方 **in the distance** 遠方に

□ **distinguish** 動①見分ける, 区別する ②特色づける ③相違を見分ける

□ **distinguishable** 形区別できる

□ **distorted** 形ゆがめられた, 歪曲された **become distorted** ゆがむ

□ **distortion** 名歪曲, ゆがめること

□ **distract** 動(注意などを)そらす, まぎらす

□ **distracted by**《be –》〜に気を取られる

□ **divide** 動分かれる, 分ける, 割れる, 割る **divide up** 分ける

□ **do** 熟 **not do well** 苦手である

□ **dodge** 動さっと身をかわす, さっと隠れる

□ **dodging** 名素早く身をかわすこと

□ **dōjō** 名道場

□ **domain** 名統治地域, 領土

□ **door** 熟 **sliding door** 引き戸, 襖

□ **double** 形①2倍の, 二重の ②対の 動2倍になる[する]

□ **doubt** 名①疑い, 不確かなこと ②未解決点, 困難 動疑う

□ **down** 熟 **be broken down into** 〜に分解される **be set down on paper** 紙に書き留められている **bear down on** 〜を威圧する **bring down** 打ち降ろす, 仕留める **come down in the world** 落ちぶれる **cut down** 切り倒す, 打ちのめす **hang down** ぶら下がる **loaded down with** 〜で手一杯である **look down upon** 見下ろす, 俯瞰する **pass down** (次の世代に)伝える **put down in writing** 書き物にする, 書き留める **set down** 〜を下に置く, 〜と見なす **turn down** 伏せる **write down** 書き留める

□ **downward** 形下方の, 下向きの, 下降する, 以後の

□ **dozen** 名1ダース, 12(個)

□ **drag** 動引きずる

□ **dragged into** 《be ~》引きずり込まれる

□ **drama** 名劇, 演劇, ドラマ, 劇的な事件

□ **draw** 動①引く, 引っ張る ②描く ③引き分けになる[する]

□ **drive back** (敵などを)追い返す

□ **drive off** 撃退する

□ **duel** 名決闘, 勝負

□ **dull** 形退屈な, 鈍い, くすんだ, ぼんやりした **grow dull** (切れ味が)鈍る

□ **durable** 形永続する, 耐久性のある

□ **duty** 名①義務(感), 責任 ②職務, 任務, 関税

□ **dying** 動 die (死ぬ)の現在分詞

E

□ **each other** お互いに

□ **earnest** 形熱心な, 真剣な, 重大な

□ **earnestly** 副まじめに

□ **ease** 名安心, 気楽 **at ease** ゆとりがあって

□ **easily** 副①容易に, たやすく, 苦もなく ②気楽に

□ **edge** 名①刃 ②端, 縁

□ **effect** 名①影響, 効果, 結果 ②実施, 発効

□ **effective** 形効果的である, 有効である

□ **effectively** 副効果的に, 効率的に

□ **efficiency** 名①能率, 効率 ②能力

□ **efficient** 形①効率的な, 有効な ②有能な, 敏腕な

□ **efficiently** 副効果的に, 能率的に

□ **either A or B** Aかそれともв B

□ **elbow** 名ひじ

□ **elevation** 名①高める[高められる]こと, 昇進 ②標高

□ **else** 副 **above all else** とりわけ, 何にもまして

□ **embody** 動具体化する, 具体的に表現する

□ **embrace** 動抱き締める

□ **emerge** 動現れる, 浮かび上がる, 明らかになる

□ **emphasis** 名強調, 強勢, 重要性

□ **emphasize** 動①強調する ②重視する

□ **employ** 動①(人を)雇う, 使う ②利用する

□ **emptiness** 名①から, 空虚, 無意味 ②空腹

□ **enable** 動 (~することを)可能にする, 容易にする

□ **encirclement** 名包囲

□ **encompass** 動~を包含する

□ **encounter** 動(思いがけなく)出会う, 遭う 名遭遇, (思いがけない)出会い

□ **encourage** 動①勇気づける ②促進する, 助長する

□ **encouragement** 名激励, 励み, 促進

□ **end** 熟 **end up** 結局~になる **in the end** とうとう, 結局, ついに

□ **endeavor** 名努力

□ **enemy** 名敵

□ **engage** 動①約束する, 婚約する ②雇う, 従事する[させる], 《be -d in》~に従事している **engage in** ~に従事する

□ **engagement** 名婚約, 約束 **large engagement** 合戦

□ **engraving** 名彫り込み

□ **enlarge** 動①大きくなる, 増大する ②詳細に述べる ③拡大する, 増大させる

□ **enough to do** ~するのに十分な

Word List

- ☐ **ensure** 動 確実にする, 保証する

- ☐ **entail** 動 (必然的に) 伴う, 含む, 必要とする

- ☐ **entangle** 動 (面倒なことに) 巻き込む, もつれさせる **be entangled** 絡まる, もつれる **become entangled** もつれる, 絡まる

- ☐ **entanglement** 名 絡み合い

- ☐ **entirely** 副 完全に, まったく

- ☐ **entryway** 名 通路, 通用門 **entryway into** ～の中への通路

- ☐ **equal** 形 等しい, 均等な, 平等な **on equal terms with** ～と同じ条件で, ～と対等で

- ☐ **equally** 副 等しく, 平等に

- ☐ **equipment** 名 装置, 機材, 道具, 設備

- ☐ **equivalent** 形 ①同等の, 等しい ②同意義の **be equivalent to** ～と等しい, ～に相当する

- ☐ **era** 名 時代, 年代

- ☐ **erase** 動 ①消える ②消去する, 抹消する

- ☐ **erratic** 形 気まぐれな, 一貫性のない

- ☐ **error** 名 誤り, 間違い, 過失

- ☐ **essence** 名 ①本質, 真髄, 最重要点 ②エッセンス, エキス

- ☐ **essential** 形 本質的な, 必須の 名 本質, 要点, 必需品

- ☐ **establish** 動 確立する, 立証する, 設置 [設立] する

- ☐ **establishment** 名 ①確立, 設立, 発足 ②《the E-》体制

- ☐ **etiquette** 名 エチケット, 礼儀 (作法)

- ☐ **evade** 動 回避する, 巧みに避ける

- ☐ **evasion** 名 逃れること

- ☐ **even if** たとえ～でも

- ☐ **even then** その時でさえ

- ☐ **even though** ～であるけれども, ～にもかかわらず

- ☐ **eventually** 副 結局は

- ☐ **every time** ～するときはいつも

- ☐ **everyday** 形 毎日の, 日々の

- ☐ **everyone** 代 誰でも, 皆

- ☐ **everything** 代 すべてのこと [もの], 何でも, 何もかも

- ☐ **everywhere** 副 どこにいても, いたるところに

- ☐ **evil** 形 邪悪な

- ☐ **exact** 形 正確な, 厳密な, きちょうめんな

- ☐ **examine** 動 試験する, 調査 [検査] する, 診察する

- ☐ **example** 熟 **for example** たとえば

- ☐ **exasperate** 動 憤慨させる, 怒らせる, いらいらさせる

- ☐ **exasperated** 形 憤慨して, いら立って

- ☐ **exceptional** 形 例外的な, 特別に優れた

- ☐ **exclusive** 形 排他的な, 独占的な

- ☐ **execute** 動 実行する, 執行する

- ☐ **exhausted** 形 疲れ切った, 消耗した

- ☐ **exhibit** 動 展示する, 見せる, 示す **exhibit a change** 変化を見せる

- ☐ **exist** 動 存在する, 生存する, ある, いる

- ☐ **exit** 名 出口

- ☐ **expect** 動 予期 [予測] する, (当然のこととして) 期待する

- ☐ **expeditious** 形 迅速な

- ☐ **expert** 名 専門家, 熟練者, エキスパート

- ☐ **explanation** 名 ①説明, 解説, 釈明 ②解釈, 意味

- ☐ **explore** 動 探検 [調査] する, 切り開く

- ☐ **expression** 名 表現, 表示, 表情

- ☐ **extended** 形 伸ばされた, 引き伸

A
B
C
D
E
F
G
H
I
J
K
L
M
N
O
P
Q
R
S
T
U
V
W
X
Y
Z

ばされた, 広げられた

- **extent** 名範囲, 程度, 広さ, 広がり
- **extract** 動引き抜く
- **extracted** 形抜く, 抜き取る
- **extremely** 副非常に, 極度に
- **eye** 熟 discerning eye 鑑識眼 keep an eye on ～から目を離さない keep an observant eye on ～をずっと注視する
- **eyeball** 名眼球
- **eyebrow** 名まゆ(眉)

F

- **fact** 熟 in fact つまり, 実は, 要するに
- **factor** 名要因, 要素, 因子
- **fail** 動①失敗する, 落第する[させる] ②《 – to ～》～し損なう, ～できない ③失望させる
- **failing** 名欠点, 弱点
- **fall** 名没落, 衰退 熟 fall behind 取り残される, 後れを取る fall into 急に～になる, ～に陥る, ～してしまう fall upon ～に向かって行く, ～の上にかかる
- **false** 形うその, 間違った, にせの, 不誠実な
- **falter** 動ためらう, くじける
- **familiar** 形①親しい, 親密な ②《 be – with ～》～に精通している, ～をよく知っている, ～と親しい ③普通の, いつもの, おなじみの
- **fancy** 形装飾的な, 見事な
- **far** 熟 as far as ～と同じくらい遠く, ～まで, ～に関する限りは go far 遠くへ行く
- **fathom** 動推測する, 見抜く
- **favor** 動～の方を好む
- **favorable** 形好意的な, 都合のよい

- **favored** 形気に入られている
- **fear** 名①恐れ ②心配, 不安 put fear into ～を恐怖で縮み上がらせる
- **feature** 名特徴, 特色
- **feeling** 名①感じ, 気持ち ②触感, 知覚 ③同情, 思いやり, 感受性
- **feint** 動偽る, ふりをする 名フェイント, 陽動
- **fell** 熟 in one fell swoop 一挙に
- **fend** 動(攻撃・質問などを)かわす, 受け流す fend off 払いのける, かわす
- **field** 熟 rice field 田
- **fight** 熟 fight with ～と戦う in a fight with ～と戦っている
- **fighter** 名戦士
- **fighting** 名戦闘 hand-to-hand fighting 白兵戦
- **figure** 熟 the thumb and the index figure 親指と人差し指《figure はここでは指の一部を表わす》
- **filled with** 《 be – 》～でいっぱいになる
- **fineness** 名細かさ, 微妙さ
- **finer details** 細部
- **firewood** 名まき, たき木
- **firing** 名(銃の)点火, 発砲
- **firm** 形しっかりした, 断固とした 動しっかりと
- **firmly** 副しっかりと, 断固として
- **firmness** 名堅固, 堅さ
- **first** 熟 at first 最初は, 初めのうちは for the first time 初めて
- **fish** 熟 a school of fish 魚の群れ
- **fist** 名こぶし, げんこつ
- **fit** 形適当な, 相応な 動合致[適合]する, 合致させる
- **fix** 動①固定する[させる] ②修理する ③決定する ④用意する, 整える fix on ～にくぎ付けになる
- **fixated** 形(～に)執着した

become fixated on ～に執着している

□ **fixed** 形固定した, ゆるぎない
  fixed form 一定の型

□ **flamboyant** 形きらびやかな, 派手な

□ **flash** 名閃光, きらめき **in a flash** すぐに

□ **flashy** 形①閃光のような ②派手な, けばけばしい

□ **flat** 名平面, 平らな部分 **flat of the sword** 刀のひら

□ **flight** 名飛ぶこと, 飛行

□ **flintstone** 名火打ち石の小石

□ **float** 動①浮く, 浮かぶ ②漂流する

□ **floating** 形流動的な, 浮遊している

□ **floor beam** 床梁

□ **flourish** 動活躍する

□ **flourishing** 形栄える

□ **flow** 名流出

□ **flowing** 形流れる, 流れている

□ **flustered** 動揺して, うろたえて
  become flustered うろたえる get flustered 動揺する

□ **follow up on** ～を実行に移す

□ **follow-up** 形後に続く

□ **followed by** その後に～が続いて

□ **following** 動follow (ついていく) の現在分詞 形《the –》次の, 次に続く

□ **fool** 動ばかにする, だます, ふざける

□ **foot soldier** 足軽

□ **footing** 名足もと, 足どり

□ **footwork** 名脚の動き, 脚さばき

□ **for** 熟 as for ～に関しては, ～はどうかと言うと call for ～を求める, 訴える, ～を呼び求める, 呼び出す care for ～の世話をする, ～を扱う, ～が好きである, ～を大事に思う for example たとえば for instance たとえば for the first time 初めて for the masses 大衆のために for the moment 差し当たり, 当座は for the sake of ～のために go for ～に出かける, ～を追い求める, ～を好む go in for ～を楽しむ, ～に熱中する make a name for oneself 名を成す[上げる], 名声を得る reason for ～の理由 show a preference for ～を好む strive for ～を得ようと努力する wait for ～を待つ what … for どんな目的で

□ **force** 名力, 勢い 動①強制する, 力ずくで～する, 余儀なく～させる ②押しやる, 押し込む force them back 力ずくで無理やり戻す

□ **forced** 形強制的な

□ **forceful** 形力強い, 説得力のある

□ **forcefully** 副力強く

□ **forehead** 名ひたい

□ **foresee** 動予見する, 見通す

□ **forge** 動形づくる, 構築する

□ **form** 名①形, 形式 ②書式 fixed form 一定の型 tangible form 有形の形式

□ **formal** 形正式の, 公式の, 形式的な, 格式ばった formal room 座敷

□ **formation** 名①形成, 編成 ②隊形, フォーメーション

□ **former** 形①前の, 先の, 以前の ②《the –》(二者のうち) 前者の

□ **formidable** 形恐ろしい, 侮りがたい

□ **fortress** 名要塞, 堅固な場所

□ **fortune** 名①富, 財産 ②幸運, 繁栄, チャンス ③運命, 運勢 make a fortune 財を成す

□ **forward** 副①前方に ②将来に向けて ③先へ, 進んで push forward 前へ進む, 突き出す thrust forward 前に突き出す

□ **fountainhead** 名《通例a [the]

127

－》源泉, 典拠

- □ **fractionally** 副 わずかに
- □ **freedom** 名 ①自由 ②束縛がないこと
- □ **freely** 副 自由に, 障害なしに
- □ **freeze** 動 ①凍る, 凍らせる ②ぞっとする[させる] **until hell freezes over** 永遠に
- □ **frequently** 副 頻繁に, しばしば
- □ **frighten** 動 驚かせる, びっくりさせる
- □ **frightened** 形 おびえた, びっくりした
- □ **from straight above** 真上から
- □ **from the perspective of** ～ の観点からすれば
- □ **front of** 熟《in －》～の前に, ～の正面に
- □ **frustrate** 動 ～をいらつかせる
- □ **frustrating** 動 frustrate (挫折させる)の現在分詞
- □ **Fujiwara** 名 藤原《人名》
- □ **full complement** 全装備
- □ **fully** 副 十分に, 完全に, まるまる
- □ **fundamental** 名 基本, 原理 形 基本の, 根本的な, 重要な
- □ **fundamentally** 副 根本[根源]的に
- □ **further** 形 いっそう遠い, その上の, なおいっそうの 副 いっそう遠く, その上に, もっと
- □ **furthermore** 副 さらに, その上

G

- □ **gagaku** 名 雅楽
- □ **gain** 動 ①得る, 増す ②進歩する, 進む
- □ **gap** 名 ギャップ, 隔たり, すき間
- □ **gather** 動 ①集まる, 集める ②生

じる, 増す ③推測する

- □ **general** 形 全体の, 一般の, 普通の **general description** 概要 名 一般 **in general** 一般に, たいてい
- □ **generally** 副 ①一般に, だいたい ②たいてい
- □ **get accustomed to** ～に慣れる
- □ **get frustered** 動揺する
- □ **get in** 中に入る, 乗り込む **get in close** 入り込む
- □ **get used to** ～になじむ, ～に慣れる
- □ **giant** 形 巨大な
- □ **give up** あきらめる, やめる, 引き渡す
- □ **go** 熟 **come and go** 行き交う, 去来する, 移り変わる **go amiss** (物事が)順調にいかない **go far** 遠くへ行く **go for** ～に出かける, ～を追い求める, ～を好む **go in for** ～を楽しむ, ～に熱中する **go into** ～に入る **go into detail** 詳しく[詳細に]述べる[説明する] **go on** 続く, 続ける, 進み続ける, 起こる, 発生する **go on to** ～に移る, ～に取り掛かる **go through** 通り抜ける, 一つずつ順番に検討する **go wrong** 失敗する, 道を踏みはずす, 調子が悪くなる
- □ **goggle** 動 目をむく
- □ **good** 熟 **not good at all** お話にならない
- □ **govern** 動 治める, 管理する, 支配する
- □ **grab** 動 ふいにつかむ
- □ **gradually** 副 だんだんと
- □ **grapple** 動 組み合う
- □ **grappling** 名 組み技
- □ **grasp** 動 つかむ, 握る, とらえる, 理解する **grasp the meaning** 意味を把握する
- □ **grooved** 形 溝付きの **grooved beam** 鴨居

- □ **ground** 熟 on the ground 地面に
- □ **grow dull** (切れ味が) 鈍る
- □ **guard** 名 守り, 防御
- □ **guideline** 名 ガイドライン, 指針
- □ **gust** 名 突風

H

- □ **habit** 名 習慣, 癖, 気質
- □ **habitually** 副 習慣的に
- □ **hail** 動 (出身地から) 来る, (国元から) 出て来る hail from ～の出身である
- □ **halberd** 名 長刀
- □ **halberdier** 名 長刀使い
- □ **half-baked** 形 生半可な, 中途半端な
- □ **half-hearted** 形 いいかげんな気持ちの, 及び腰の, 身が入らない
- □ **hall** 名 公会堂, ホール, 大広間, 玄関
- □ **hand** 熟 at hand 近くに, 目前に, すぐ使えるように hand in hand 手をとり合って have the upper hand 有利[優勢]である on the other hand 一方, 他方では
- □ **hand-to-hand** 形 (戦いなどが) 至近距離での hand-to-hand fighting 白兵戦
- □ **handle** 動 操縦する, 取り扱う
- □ **handling** 名 取り扱い, 処理
- □ **handsome** 形 端正な (顔立ちの), りっぱな, (男性が) ハンサムな
- □ **hang** 動 かかる, かける, つるす, ぶら下げる hang down ぶら下がる
- □ **happening** 名 出来事, 事件
- □ **harbor** 名 港
- □ **hard to** ～し難い
- □ **Harima** 名 播磨の国《地名, 現在の兵庫県南西部》
- □ **harmful** 形 害を及ぼす, 有害な

- □ **harmless** 形 無害の, 安全な
- □ **harmony** 名 調和, 一致, ハーモニー in harmony with ～と調和して
- □ **have** 熟 could have done ～だったかもしれない《仮定法》 have no intention of ～する気はない have no time to do ～する時間がない have the upper hand 有利[優勢]である
- □ **hawk** 名 タカ (鷹)
- □ **haze** 名 かすみ, もや
- □ **head** 熟 head of ～の長 pop into someone's head (考えが) ひょいと頭に浮かぶ
- □ **head-on** 副 真っ正面から attack head-on 正面から攻撃する
- □ **healing** 形 治療の, 病気を治す, いやす
- □ **heart** 熟 in one's heart of hearts 内心は
- □ **heaven** 名 天国
- □ **heel** 名 ①かかと, ヒール ②(動物の) 後ろ足
- □ **height** 名 ①高さ, 身長 ②《the - 》絶頂, 真っ盛り ③高台, 丘
- □ **hell** 名 地獄, 地獄のようなところ[状態] until hell freezes over 永遠に
- □ **herd** 名 (大型動物の) 一群, 群集, 民衆
- □ **here and there** あちこちで
- □ **here is ～** こちらは～です。
- □ **heretofore** 副 これまで
- □ **hesitant** 形 ちゅうちょする, ためらいがちな
- □ **hesitation** 名 ためらい, ちゅうちょ without hesitation ちゅうちょなく
- □ **hey** 間 ①《呼びかけ・注意を促して》おい, ちょっと ②へえ, おや, まあ
- □ **hidden** 形 隠れた, 秘密の
- □ **hide** 動 隠れる, 隠す, 隠れて見えない, 秘密にする hide out (犯人など

が) 潜伏している

□ **Higo** 名 肥後の国《地名, 現在の熊本県》

□ **hilt** 名 (剣の) つか

□ **hindrance** 名 妨害, じゃま, 障害物

□ **hit it off with** (人) と折り合う, ～とうまくやる

□ **Hitachi** 名 常陸の国《地名, 現在の茨城県》

□ **hold back** (事実・本心などを) 隠す, (感情を) 抑える, 自制する, 引き下がる

□ **hone** 動 ～を砥石で研ぐ **hone one's skills** 自分の技 (能) を磨く

□ **honed** 形 研ぎ澄まされた

□ **honestly** 副 正直に

□ **honor** 名 名誉, 光栄, 信用 **seat of honor** 上席

□ **hopelessly** 副 希望を失って, どうしようもなく

□ **hopping** 形 飛び回っている, 次から次へと移動する

□ **horizontally** 副 水平に

□ **horseback** 名 馬の背

□ **household** 名 家族, 世帯

□ **how** 熟 **no matter how** どんなに～であろうとも

□ **however** 副 たとえ～でも 接 けれども, だが

□ **huge** 形 巨大な, ばく大な

□ **hurried** 形 急いでした, せきたてられた

I

□ **ideal** 形 理想的な, 申し分のない

□ **if** 熟 **as if** あたかも～のように, まるで～みたいに **even if** たとえ～でも **if possible** できるなら

□ **ignorant** 形 ①無知な, 無学な ②知らないで, 気づかないで

□ **ignorantly** 副 知らないで

□ **imitate** 動 まねる, 模造する

□ **immediate** 形 さっそくの, 即座の, 直接の

□ **immediately** 副 すぐに, ～するやいなや

□ **immovable** 形 動かせない, 動くことができない

□ **importance** 名 重要性, 大切さ

□ **improve** 動 改善する [させる], 進歩する

□ **in** 熟 **in a fight with** ～と戦っている **in a flash** すぐに **in a way** ある意味では **in accordance with** ～に従って **in addition** 加えて, さらに **in all of which** それら全ての中で **in any case** とにかく **in any way** 決して, 多少なりとも **in attempting to** ～しようとして 手短に **in contrast to** ～と大いに異なって **in disarray** 混乱して **in fact** つまり, 実は, 要するに **in front of** ～の前に, ～の正面に **in general** 一般に, たいてい **in harmony with** ～と調和して **in one direction** 同一の方向に **in one fell swoop** 一挙に **in one's heart of hearts** 内心は **in order** きちんと (整理されて), 順序正しく **in order to** ～するために, ～しようと **in other words** すなわち, 言い換えれば **in particular** 特に, とりわけ **in proportion to** ～に比例して **in reference to** ～に関して **in regard to** ～に関しては **in search of** ～を探し求めて **in short** 要約すると **in terms of** ～の言葉で言えば, ～の点から **in that context** その意味で **in that regard** そのことについて **in the case of** ～の場合は **in the distance** 遠方に **in the end** とうとう, 結局, ついに **in the least** 少しも **in the middle of** ～の真ん中 [中ほど] に **in the midst of** ～の真っただ中に **in the world** 世界で **in the world at large** 世界中に広く **in the world of business** 商売の世界

では **in this way** このようにして **in time** 間に合って, やがて **in writing** 書面で

□ **inaccurate** 形 不正確な, いい加減な

□ **inadvertent** 形 不注意な, うっかりした

□ **incapable** 形 (〜が) できない, 無資格の

□ **incline** 動 傾ける, 傾く, 曲げる 名 傾斜(面) **steep incline** 急勾配

□ **include** 動 含む, 勘定に入れる

□ **including** 前 〜を含めて, 込みで

□ **incompatible** 形 相容れない, 両立しない, 矛盾した **be incompatible with** 〜と相いれない

□ **inconvenient** 形 不便な, 不自由な

□ **incorrect** 形 正しくない, 間違った

□ **indecisive** 形 どっちつかずの

□ **indeed** 副 実際, 本当に

□ **index** 名 ①索引 ②しるし, 現れ ③指数 **index finger** 人さし指 **the thumb and the index figure** 親指と人差し指《figure はここでは指の一部を表わす》

□ **indicate** 動 ①指す, 示す, (道などを) 教える ②それとなく言う ③きざしがある

□ **indistinguishable** 形 区別ができない

□ **individual** 形 独立した, 個性的な, 個々の 名 個体, 個人

□ **indoors** 副 室内で, 屋内で

□ **inexperienced** 形 経験のない, 不慣れな

□ **inextricably** 副 切り離せないほどに, 密接に, 緊密に

□ **inferior** 形 (質の) 劣った, 下位の, 粗悪な **inferior to** 〜より劣っている

□ **influence** 動 影響をおよぼす

□ **initial** 形 最初の, 初めの

□ **initiative** 名 主導権, イニシアチブ **take the initiative** 先手を打つ **take the initiative in** 〜においてイニシアチブ[主導権]を取る

□ **injury** 名 けが

□ **ink** 名 インク

□ **inner** 形 ①内部の ②心の中の **inner meaning** 奥義 **inner secret** 奥義

□ **insist** 動 ①主張する, 断言する ②要求する

□ **instance** 名 ①例 ②場合, 事実 **for instance** たとえば

□ **instant** 名 瞬間, 寸時 **the instant of** 〜の拍子

□ **instantly** 副 すぐに, 即座に

□ **instead** 副 その代わりに **instead of** 〜の代わりに, 〜をしないで

□ **instruct** 動 ①教える, 教育する ②指図[命令]する

□ **instruction** 名 教えること, 指示, 助言

□ **instructive** 形 教育的な, 有益な, ためになる

□ **intellectual** 形 知的な, 知性のある **intellectual notion** 知的概念

□ **intend** 動 《– to 〜》〜しようと思う, 〜するつもりである

□ **intended** 形 意図された

□ **intent** 名 意図, 意向

□ **intention** 名 ①意図, (〜する) つもり ②心構え **have no intention of** 〜する気はない

□ **interrupt** 動 さえぎる, 妨害する, 口をはさむ

□ **intimidate** 動 おどして〜させる, おどす

□ **into** 熟 **be broken down into** 〜に分解される **be dragged into** 引きずり込まれる **entryway into** 〜の中への通路 **fall into** 急に〜になる, 〜に陥る, 〜してしまう **go into**

The Book of Five Rings

□ **intoxication** 图酔った状態

~に入る **go into detail** 詳しく［詳細に］述べる［説明する］ **look into** ①～を検討する，～を研究する ②～の中を見る，～をのぞき込む **pop into someone's head** （考えが）ひょいと頭に浮かぶ **put fear into** ～を恐怖で縮み上がらせる **put into practice** 実践する **put ~ into …** ～を…の状態にする，～を…に突っ込む **put ~ into practice** ～を実践する **rush into** ～に突入する，～に駆けつける，～に駆け込む **take into consideration** ～を考慮に入れる **take ~ into consideration** ～を考慮に入れる

□ **intoxication** 图酔った状態

□ **invariably** 副相変わらず，変わることなく

□ **invent** 動①発明［考案］する ②ねつ造する

□ **invisible** 形目に見えない，表に出ない

□ **involve** 動①含む，伴う ②巻き込む，かかわらせる

□ **involved** 動 involve（含む）の過去，過去分詞 形①巻き込まれている，関連する ②入り組んだ，込み入っている

□ **irrational** 形理性のない，ばかげた

□ **irritate** 動いらいらさせる，怒らせる

□ **It is ~ of A to …** Aが…するのは～だ

□ **It may take ~ days to …** …するには～日かかるだろう

□ **item** 图項目，品目

□ **itself** 代それ自体，それ自身

J

□ **Japan** 图日本《国名》

□ **jaw** 图あご

□ **joint** 图①継ぎ目，継ぎ手 ②関節

□ **journey** 图①（遠い目的地への）旅 ②行程

□ **judge** 動判決を下す，裁く，判断する，評価する

□ **judgment** 图①判断，意見 ②裁判，判決

□ **juggle** 動曲芸をする，巧みにこなす

□ **jumble** 動混乱する

□ **just as** （ちょうど）であろうとおり

K

□ **Kan'ei** 图寛永《日本の元号の一つ。1624年から1644年まで》

□ **Kanbun** 图寛文《日本の元号の一つ。1661年から1673年まで》

□ **Kannon** 图観音菩薩

□ **Kashima Katori shrine** 鹿島香取神社

□ **katana** 图刀

□ **keep** 熟 **keep alert** 警戒を怠らない **keep an eye on** ～から目を離さない **keep an observant eye on** ～をずっと注視する **keep in tune with** ～と調子を合わせる **keep someone from** ～から（人）を阻む **keep up with** ～に遅れずについていく，～と歩調を合わせる **keep ~ in order** ～に規律を守らせる

□ **kilometer** 图キロメートル《長さの単位》

□ **kind of** ある程度，いくらか，～のようなもの［人］

□ **kindness** 图親切（な行為），優しさ

□ **knee** 图ひざ

□ **knock** 動ノックする，たたく，ぶつける **knock the bottom out** 根底から覆す

□ **knot** 图こぶ，節

□ **knotless** 形節のない

□ **knotty** 形節だらけの

□ **knowledge** 名知識, 理解, 学問

□ **knowledgeable** 形よく知っている

□ **known as** 《be –》〜として知られている

□ **kodachi** 名小太刀

□ **Kyoto** 名京都《地名》

L

□ **lack** 動不足している, 欠けている

□ **lacking** 形不足している, 欠けている be lacking in 〜が足りない

□ **lantern** 名手提げランプ, ランタン

□ **large** 熟 at large 全体として, 広く by and large 概して in the world at large 世界中に広く large engagement 合戦

□ **large-scale** 形大規模の

□ **largely** 副大いに, 主として

□ **later on** もっと後で, のちほど

□ **latter** 形《the –》後者《代名詞的に用いる》

□ **lax** 形ゆるい, 手ぬるい

□ **lay** 動置く, 横たえる, 敷く

□ **lead someone around by the nose** (人)を思うままに操る

□ **lead someone astray** (人)を道に迷わせる

□ **lead to** 〜に至る, 〜に通じる, 〜を引き起こす

□ **lean** 動①もたれる, 寄りかかる ②傾く, 傾ける

□ **leap** 動①跳ぶ ②跳び越える leap in to 〜に飛び込む

□ **learner** 名学習者, 初心者

□ **least** 名最小, 最少 in the least 少しも

□ **leave behind** あとにする, 〜を置き去りにする

□ **leave nothing undone** やり残しを残さない

□ **led** 動 lead (導く) の過去, 過去分詞 be led around by the nose (人)に翻弄される be led astray 惑わされる

□ **leeway** 名余裕

□ **left behind** 《be –》置いていかれる

□ **leisurely** 形のんびりした, くつろいだ

□ **lend** 動貸す, 貸し出す

□ **length** 名長さ, 縦, たけ, 距離

□ **lengthy** 形非常に長い, 長ったらしい

□ **less** 副〜より少なく, 〜ほどでなく much less より少ない

□ **level** 名①水平, 平面 ②水準 形①水平の, 平たい ②同等[同位] の

□ **lid** 名 (箱, なべなどの) ふた

□ **lie** 動 (ある状態に) ある, 存在する

□ **life** 熟 life or death struggle 死ぬか生きるかの戦い life threatening 生命を危うくする way of life 生き様, 生き方, 暮らし方

□ **lift** 動持ち上げる, 上がる

□ **lighting** 名照明

□ **like** 熟 like this このような, こんなふうに look like 〜のように見える, 〜に似ている would like 〜がほしい would like to 〜したいと思う

□ **likely** 形ありそうな, (〜) しそうな

□ **likewise** 副同じように

□ **limit** 名限界, 《-s》範囲, 境界

□ **line** 熟 on the line 危険にひんして, 風前の灯で

□ **list** 名名簿, 目録, 一覧表

□ **literary** 形文学の, 文芸の

□ **living** 名生計, 生活 make a living 生計を立てる, 自活する

□ **loaded** 形荷を積んだ, 詰め込んだ **loaded down with** 〜で手一杯である

□ **locale** 名現場, 場所

□ **long** 熟 **all day long** 一日中, 終日 **as long as** 〜する以上は, 〜である限りは **no longer** もはや〜でない [〜しない]

□ **look around** まわりを見回す

□ **look down upon** 見下ろす, 俯瞰する

□ **look into** ①〜を検討する, 〜を研究する ②〜の中を見る, 〜をのぞき込む

□ **look like** 〜のように見える, 〜に似ている

□ **loose** 形自由な, ゆるんだ, あいまいな

□ **looseness** 名緩み, 弛緩

□ **lord** 名首長, 主人, 領主

□ **lose sight of** 〜を見失う

□ **loss** 名①損失(額・物), 損害, 浪費 ②失敗, 敗北

□ **lower** 形もっと低い, 下級の, 劣った 動下げる, 低くする

□ **lower-ranking** 形下級の

M

□ **main** 形主な, 主要な

□ **maintain** 動①維持する ②養う

□ **make** 熟 **make a crossing** 横断をする **make a fortune** 財を成す **make a living** 生計を立てる, 自活する **make a mistake** 間違いをする **make a name for oneself** 名を成す[上げる], 名声を得る **make a plaything** 思うがままに翻弄する **make contact** 接触する **make money** お金を儲ける **make one's way** 前進する **make sense** 意味をなす, よくわかる **make use of** 〜を利用する, 〜を生かす **not make**

sense 意味をなさない

□ **maker** 名作る人, メーカー

□ **manage** 動動かす, うまく処理する

□ **maneuver** 動操る, 誘導する

□ **manner** 名①方法, やり方 ②態度, 様子 ③《-s》行儀, 作法, 生活様式

□ **mark** 名印, 記号, 跡 **miss one's mark** 的を外す

□ **marsh** 名沼地, 湿地

□ **martial arts** 武芸

□ **mass** 名固まり, (密集した)集まり **for the masses** 大衆のために

□ **master** 名主人, 雇い主, 師, 名匠 動①修得する ②〜の主となる

□ **mastery** 名支配(力) **mastery of** 〜への精通

□ **match** 名試合, 勝負 動①〜に匹敵する ②調和する, 釣り合う ③(〜を…と)勝負させる

□ **matter** 名 **a matter of** 〜の問題 **as a matter of course** 当然のことながら **matter of course** もちろんの事, 当たり前の事 **no matter** 〜を問わず, どうでもいい **no matter how** どんなに〜であろうとも **no matter what** たとえ何があろうと

□ **may** 熟 **It may take** 〜 **days to** ……するには〜日かかるだろう

□ **meaning** 名①意味, 趣旨 ②重要性 **grasp the meaning** 意味を把握する **inner meaning** 奥義

□ **means** 熟 **by means of** 〜を用いて, 〜によって **means of** 〜する手段

□ **measure** 名①寸法, 測定, 計量, 単位 ②程度, 基準

□ **measurement** 名①測定 ②寸法

□ **memory** 名記憶(力), 思い出 **commit to memory** 記憶する

□ **mental** 形①心の, 精神の ②知能[知性]の

Word List

□ **mentality** 名精神構造, メンタリティ, 考え方

□ **mentally** 副心で, 精神的に

□ **mention** 動（～について）述べる, 言及する

□ **merchant** 名商人, 貿易商

□ **merciful** 形慈悲深い

□ **merely** 副単に, たかが～に過ぎない

□ **merit** 名価値, 長所, メリット

□ **meter** 名メートル《長さの単位》

□ **method** 名①方法, 手段 ②秩序, 体系

□ **meticulous** 形きちょうめんな, 細かいことにこだわる

□ **middle** 名中間, 最中 in the middle of ～の真ん中［中ほど］に 形中間の, 中央の middle finger中指

□ **midst** 名真ん中, 中央 in the midst of ～の真っただ中に

□ **might** 助《may の過去》①～かもしれない ②～してもよい, ～できる 名力, 権力

□ **mild** 形柔和な, 温和な, 口あたりのよい, 穏やかな

□ **military** 形軍隊［軍人］の, 軍事の military strategy 軍事戦略

□ **mind** 名①心, 精神, 考え ②知性 turn ～ over in one's mind ～をよく考える 動①気にする, いやがる ②気をつける, 用心する

□ **mindful** 形心にかける, 注意して be mindful of ～を心に留める

□ **misfortune** 名不運, 不幸, 災難

□ **mishandle** 動取り扱いを誤る

□ **miss one's mark** 的を外す

□ **misshapen** 形ゆがんだ

□ **mistake** 熟 make a mistake 間違いをする

□ **mix** 動①混ざる, 混ぜる ②（～を）一緒にする mix in 混入する, よく混ぜ合わせる

□ **model** 名①模型, 設計図 ②模範

□ **modern** 形現代［近代］の, 現代的な, 最近の

□ **mold** 名型, 鋳型

□ **moment** 名①瞬間, ちょっとの間 ②（特定の）時, 時期 at that moment その時に, その瞬間に at the moment 今は for the moment 差し当たり, 当座は pause a moment 一呼吸おく

□ **momentum** 名勢い, 弾み, 推進力, 運動量

□ **money** 熟 make money お金を儲ける

□ **monkey** 名サル（猿）

□ **monotonous** 形単調な, 一本調子の

□ **mood** 名気分, 機嫌, 雰囲気, 憂うつ

□ **morale** 名士気, 意欲, やる気

□ **more** 熟 no more than ただの～にすぎない

□ **moreover** 副その上, さらに

□ **motion** 名①運動, 移動 ②身振り, 動作

□ **mouse** 名（ハツカ）ネズミ

□ **mouth** 熟 word of mouth 口頭

□ **move apart** 離れていく

□ **move in** 近寄る, 近くに来る move in close 近寄る

□ **movement** 名①動き, 運動 ②《-s》行動 ③引っ越し ④変動

□ **moving** 動 move（動く）の現在分詞 形①動いている ②感動させる

□ **Mt. Iwato** 岩戸山《長崎県南島原市にある山》

□ **much** 熟 much less まして～でない too much 過度の

□ **muscle** 名筋肉, 腕力

□ **musician** 名音楽家

□ **musket** 名鉄砲

□ **musketeer** 名鉄砲射ち

□ **myriad** 形無数の, おびただしい

□ **mysterious** 形神秘的な, 謎めいた

□ **mystery** 名①神秘, 不可思議 ②推理小説, ミステリー

N

□ **name** 熟 make a name for oneself 名を成す［上げる］, 名声を得る

□ **namely** 副すなわち, つまり

□ **narrow** 形①狭い ②限られた

□ **narrow strait** 名海峡

□ **naturally** 副生まれつき, 自然に, 当然

□ **necessarily** 副①必ず, 必然的に, やむを得ず ②《not –》必ずしも～でない

□ **necessary** 形必要な, 必然の

□ **needle** 名針

□ **needless** 形不必要な needless to say 言うまでもなく

□ **negligent** 形怠慢な, 不注意な

□ **neither** 副《否定文に続いて》～も…しない

□ **nervous** 形①神経の ②神経質な, おどおどした

□ **Ni Ten Ichi Ryū** 二天一流《宮本武蔵 が, 晩年に完成させた兵法》

□ **night** 熟 day and night 昼も夜も

□ **nip** 動①摘み取る, はさみで切り取る ②急いで行く, nip and tuck 五分五分で nip ～ in the bud ～の芽を摘む, 未然に防ぐ

□ **Nitō** 名二刀（流）

□ **Nitō Ichi Ryū** 二刀一流《二天一流の旧称。俗に二刀流と呼ばれる, 2つの刀を使う技にちなむ》

□ **no** 熟 have no intention of ～する気はない have no time to do ～する時間がない no longer もはや～でない［～しない］ no matter ～を問わず, どうでもいい no matter how どんなに～であろうとも no matter what たとえ何があろうと no more than ただの～にすぎない no one 誰も［一人も］～ない there is no way ～する見込みはない

□ **noble** 形気高い, 高貴な, りっぱな, 高貴な

□ **Noh** 名能楽

□ **non-visible** 形目に見えない

□ **none** 代（～の）何も［誰も・少しも］…ない

□ **nonetheless** 副それでもなお, それにもかかわらず

□ **nor** 接～もまたない neither ～ nor … ～も…もない

□ **norm** 名基準, 規範

□ **normal** 形普通の, 平均の, 標準的な

□ **nose** 熟 be led around by the nose（人）に翻弄される lead someone around by the nose（人）を思うままに操る nose ridge 鼻筋

□ **not** 熟 not do well 苦手である not good at all お話にならない not make sense 意味をなさない not only ～ but also … ～だけでなく…もまた not … without ～ ing ～せずには…しない, ～すれば必ず…する not ～ at all 少しも［全然］～ない not ～ but … …ではなくて…

□ **note** 名①メモ, 覚え書き ②注釈 動①書き留める ②注意［注目］する

□ **nothing** 熟 leave nothing undone やり残しを残さない nothing but ただ～だけ, ～にすぎない, ～のほかは何も…ない

□ **notion** 名観念, 概念, 意志 intellectual notion 知的概念

□ **novice** 名初心者, 見習い

□ **now** 熟 by now 今のところ, 今ごろまでには now and then ときどき

□ **number of** 《a－》いくつかの~, 多くの~

□ **numerous** 形 多数の

O

□ **observant** 形 すぐ気がつく, 目ざとい keep an observant eye on ~をずっと注視する

□ **observe** 動 ①観察[観測]する, 監視[注視]する ②気づく ③守る, 遵守する

□ **obsessed with** 熟 《be －》~で頭がいっぱいである

□ **obstacle** 名 障害(物), じゃま(な物)

□ **obstruct** 動 塞ぐ, 遮る

□ **occasion** 名 ①場合, (特定の)時 ②機会, 好機 ③理由, 根拠

□ **occupation** 名 ①職業, 仕事, 就業 ②占有, 居住, 占領

□ **occur** 動 (事が)起こる, 生じる, (考えなどが)浮かぶ

□ **of course** もちろん, 当然

□ **of one's own** 自分自身の

□ **of which** ~の中で

□ **off** 熟 catch someone off balance (人)の意表を突く drive off 撃退する fend off 払いのける, かわす hit it off with (人)と折り合う, ~とうまくやる pass oneself off as 自分が~になりすます push off 去る, 帰る throw ~ off balance ~の平衡[均衡]を失わせる timing is off タイミングがずれている ward off 回避する, 防ぐ, かわす

□ **offense** 名 攻撃

□ **offer** 動 申し出る, 申し込む, 提供する

□ **Oimatsu** 名 老松《能の曲目》

□ **olden** 形 昔の

□ **on** 熟 and so on ~など, その他もろもろ be set down on paper 紙に書き留められている bear down on ~を威圧する become fixated on ~に執着している carry on ①続ける ②持ち運ぶ depend on ~をあてにする, ~しだいである fix on ~にくぎ付けになる follow up on ~を実行に移す go on 続く, 続ける, 進み続ける, 起こる, 発生する go on to ~に移る, ~に取り掛かる keep an eye on ~から目を離さない keep an observant eye on ~をずっと注視する later on もっと後で, のちほど on equal terms with ~と同じ条件で, ~と対等で on the ground 地面に on the line 危険にひんして, 風前の灯で on the other hand 一方, 他方では on the spot その場で, ただちに on the surface 表向きは, うわべは on the verge of 今にも~しようとして pass on ①通り過ぎる ②(情報などを他者に)伝える put on a show 見せつける, 誇示する put one's thoughts on paper 自分の考えを紙に書き留める rely on ~を当てにする, ~を頼りにする turn one's back on ~に背を向ける, ~を無視する work on ~で働く, ~に取り組む, ~を説得する, ~に効く

□ **once** 熟 all at once いっせいに, 突然, 出し抜けに at once すぐに, 同時に

□ **one** 熟 at one time or another (正確な日付は覚えていないが)いつだったか in one direction 同一の方向に in one fell swoop 一挙に no one 誰も[一人も]~ない one day (過去の)ある日, (未来の)いつか

□ **one-foot** 形 一尺の

□ **one-on-one** 形 副 マンツーマンの[で], 一対一の[で]

□ **only** 熟 not only ~ but also … ~だけでなく…もまた

□ **opening** 名 ①開始, 始め ②開いた所, 穴

A
B
C
D
E
F
G
H
I
J
K
L
M
N
O
P
Q
R
S
T
U
V
W
X
Y
Z

- □ **openwork** 名 透かし細工
- □ **opponent** 名 敵, 反対者
- □ **opportunity** 名 好機, 適当な時期 [状況]
- □ **opposing** 形 対立[敵対]する
- □ **oral** 形 口の, 口頭の **oral transmission** 口伝
- □ **orally** 副 口頭で, 口述で **be transmitted orally** 口伝される
- □ **order** 熟 **in order** きちんと(整理されて), 順序正しく **in order to ~** するために, ~しようと **keep ~ in order** ~に規律を守らせる
- □ **ordinary** 形 ①普通の, 通常の ②並の, 平凡な
- □ **original** 形 ①始めの, 元の, 本来の ②独創的な
- □ **other** 熟 **each other** お互いに **in other words** すなわち, 言い換えれば **on the other hand** 一方, 他方では
- □ **out** 熟 **bring out** (物)をとりだす, 引き出す **burst out with** (感情を)急に表す, 激発する **carry out** 実行[遂行]する **come out** 出てくる, 出掛ける, 姿を現す **hide out** (犯人などが)潜伏している **knock the bottom out** 根底から覆す **out of** ~から外へ, ~から抜け出して **out of place** 本来あるべき場所から外れている, 場違いである **ride out the crisis** 危機を乗り切る **set out to ~** に着手する, ~し始める, ~しようと試みる **shift out of** ~から移動する **stretch out** ①手足を伸ばす, 背伸びする ②広がる **thrust out** ~を突き出す
- □ **outlier** 名 部外者
- □ **outline** 名 ①外形, 輪郭 ②概略
- □ **outstanding** 形 突出した, 際立った
- □ **outward** 形 ①外側の ②外見の
- □ **over** 熟 **all over** ~中で, 全体に亘って, ~の至る所で, 全て終わって,

もうだめで **over and over** 何度も繰り返して **turn ~ over in one's mind** ~をよくよく考える **until hell freezes over** 永遠に

- □ **overall** 形 総体的な, 全面的な **overall condition** 概況 副 全般的に見れば
- □ **overdo** 動 やりすぎる, 使いすぎる
- □ **overestimate** 動 過大評価する, 買いかぶる
- □ **overexert** 動 (精を)出し過ぎる, (労力を)使い過ぎる
- □ **overflowing** 形 あふれる, みなぎる, ほとばしる
- □ **overly** 副 過度に
- □ **overreach oneself** 無理[実力以上のこと]をしようとして失敗する
- □ **own** 熟 **of one's own** 自分自身の

P

- □ **painstaking** 形 骨の折れる, 念入りな
- □ **palace** 名 宮殿, 大邸宅
- □ **palm** 名 手のひら(状のもの)
- □ **paper** 熟 **be set down on paper** 紙に書き留められている **put one's thoughts on paper** 自分の考えを紙に書き留める
- □ **parry** 動 かわす, 受け流す
- □ **part** 熟 **play a part** 役目を果たす
- □ **particular** 形 ①特別の ②詳細な 名 事項, 細部, 《-s》詳細 **in particular** 特に, とりわけ
- □ **particularly** 副 特に, とりわけ
- □ **pass down** (次の世代に)伝える
- □ **pass on** ①通り過ぎる ②(情報などを他者に)伝える
- □ **pass oneself off as** 自分が~になりすます
- □ **passage** 名 ①通過, 通行, 通路 ②一節, 経過

□ **passing** 動pass（過ぎる）の現在分詞 形通り過ぎる, 一時的な

□ **past** 形過去の, この前の 名過去（の出来事）前《時間・場所》〜を過ぎて, 〜を越して 副通り越して, 過ぎて

□ **path** 名進路, 通路

□ **pattern** 名柄, 型, 模様

□ **pause** 名①（活動の）中止, 休止 ②区切り 動休止する, 立ち止まる **pause a moment** 一呼吸おく

□ **pay** 動①支払う, 払う, 報いる, 償う ②割に合う, ペイする **pay attention to** 〜に注意を払う

□ **peasant** 名農民, 小作人

□ **penetrate** 動①貫く, 浸潤する ②見抜く

□ **penetration** 名貫通, 浸透, 洞察

□ **perfection** 名完全, 完成

□ **perfectly** 副完全に, 申し分なく **perfectly timed** 完璧にタイミングが合っている

□ **perform** 動①（任務などを）行う, 果たす, 実行する ②演じる, 演奏する

□ **performer** 名実行者, 行為者, 上演者, 演奏者, 役者, 曲芸師

□ **perpetuation** 名永続化

□ **persevere** 動がんばって〜する, 根気よくやり通す

□ **persistent** 形①しつこい, 頑固な ②持続する, 永続的な

□ **persistently** 副持続的に, 粘り強く

□ **personal** 形①個人の, 私的な ②本人自らの

□ **perspective** 名①遠近法 ②観点 ③見通し **broader perspective** 大局的見地 **from the perspective of** 〜の観点からすれば

□ **persuade** 動説得する, 促して〜させる

□ **pheasant** 名キジ（雄）《鳥》

□ **physical** 形①物質の, 物理学の, 自然科学の ②身体の, 肉体の **physical contact** 身体的接触

□ **physically** 副①自然法則上, 物理的に ②肉体的に, 身体的に

□ **pick up** 拾い上げる, 習得する, 再開する, 回復する

□ **picture** 熟take a big picture 全体像を捉える

□ **pillar** 名①柱, 支柱, 支え ②根幹

□ **pillow** 名まくら

□ **pivot** 動〜を回転させる

□ **place** 熟out of place 本来あるべき場所から外れている, 場違いである **take place** 行われる, 起こる

□ **placement** 名配置

□ **plane** 名かんな

□ **planing** 名（木材の）平削り

□ **play a part** 役目を果たす

□ **plaything** 名①おもちゃ ②おもちゃにされる人 **make a plaything** 思うがままに翻弄する

□ **pledge** 名①誓約, 約束 ②担保 動誓約する[させる], 誓う, 保障する

□ **poetry** 名詩歌, 詩を書くこと

□ **point** 熟at this point 現在のところ **point of view** 考え方, 視点 **primary point** 主要点

□ **polish** 動磨く, つやを出す, 磨きをかける **polish one's skills** 腕を磨く

□ **pop** 動ポンと鳴る **pop into someone's head** （考えが）ひょいと頭に浮かぶ

□ **position** 名①位置, 場所, 姿勢 ②地位, 身分, 職 ③立場, 状況 **static position** 静止位置 動置く, 配置する

□ **possess** 動①持つ, 所有する ②（心などを）保つ, 制御する

□ **possibility** 名可能性, 見込み, 将来性

139

- **possible** 形 ①可能な ②ありうる, 起こりうる **as ~ as possible** できるだけ~ **if possible** できるなら
- **posture** 名 姿勢
- **pot** 名 壺, (深い)なべ
- **powerful** 形 力強い, 実力のある, 影響力のある
- **powerfully** 副 強力に, 強烈に
- **practically** 副 ①事実上, 実質的に ②ほとんど
- **practice** 熟 **put into practice** 実践する **put ~ into practice** ~を実践する
- **pray to** ~に祈る
- **precedent** 名 前例, 先例, 判例
- **precisely** 副 正確に, ちょうど
- **predict** 動 予測[予想]する
- **predisposed** 形 傾向がある
- **predisposition** 名 (~しやすい・~に陥りやすい)傾向, 性質
- **prefer** 動 (~のほうを)好む, (~のほうが)よいと思う
- **preference** 名 好きであること, 好み **show a preference for** ~を好む
- **prepared** 形 準備[用意]のできた
- **present-day** 形 今日の
- **preserve** 動 保存[保護]する, 保つ
- **press** 動 ①圧する, 押す, プレスする ②強要する, 迫る
- **pressure** 名 プレッシャー, 圧力, 圧縮, 重荷 **apply pressure** 圧力をかける
- **pretend** 動 ①ふりをする, 装う ②あえて~しようとする
- **prevail** 動 ①普及する ②勝つ, 圧倒する
- **prevent** 動 ①妨げる, じゃまする ②予防する, 守る, 《~ from …》~が…できない[しない]ようにする
- **prevention** 名 防止, 予防

- **previous** 形 前の, 先の
- **previously** 副 あらかじめ, 以前に[は]
- **priest** 名 聖職者, 牧師, 僧侶
- **primary** 形 第一の, 主要な, 最初の, 初期の **primary point** 主要点
- **principal** 名 主役, 主犯, 本人
- **principle** 名 ①原理, 原則 ②道義, 正道
- **probably** 副 たぶん, あるいは
- **proceed** 動 進む, 進展する, 続ける
- **prodigiously** 副 並外れて
- **product** 名 ①製品, 産物 ②成果, 結果
- **proficiency** 名 熟達
- **profit** 名 利益, 利潤, ため
- **progress** 名 進歩, 前進
- **progressively** 副 漸進的に
- **proper** 形 適した, 適切な, 正しい
- **properly** 副 適切に, きっちりと
- **proportion** 名 ①割合, 比率, 分け前 ②釣り合い, 比例 **in proportion to** ~に比例して
- **protruding** 形 突き出ている
- **prove** 動 ①証明する ②(~であることが)わかる, (~と)なる
- **provide** 動 ①供給する, 用意する, (~に)備える ②規定する
- **punishment** 名 ①罰, 処罰 ②罰を受けること
- **pure** 形 ①純粋な, 混じりけのない ②罪のない, 清い
- **purely** 副 まったくの, 単に, 純粋に
- **purity** 名 汚れのないこと, 清浄, 純粋, 純度
- **pursue** 動 ①追う, つきまとう ②追求する, 従事する
- **pursuit** 名 追跡, 追求
- **push against** ~を押す

Word List

- □ **push back** 押し返す，押しのける
- □ **push off** 前へ進む，突き出す
- □ **push up** 押し上げる
- □ **put** 熟 **put back** (もとの場所に) 戻す，返す **put down in writing** 書き物にする，書き留める **put fear into** ～を恐怖で縮み上がらせる **put into practice** 実践する **put on a show** 見せつける，誇示する **put one's thoughts on paper** 自分の考えを紙に書き留める **put ～ into …** ～を…の状態にする，～を…に突っ込む

Q

- □ **quality** 名 ①質，性質，品質 ②特性 ③良質
- □ **quarter** 熟 **at close quarters** 間近に，接近して
- □ **quickly** 副 敏速に，急いで
- □ **quietly** 副 ①静かに ②平穏に，控えめに
- □ **quirk** 名 ①癖，奇癖 ②気まぐれ，思いがけない出来事

R

- □ **raise** 動 ①上げる，高める ②起こす
- □ **rapid** 形 速い，急な，すばやい
- □ **rarely** 副 めったに～しない，まれに，珍しいほど
- □ **rather** 副 ①むしろ，かえって ②かなり，いくぶん，やや ③それどころか逆に **rather than** ～よりむしろ
- □ **rational** 形 理性的な，合理的な
- □ **rationale** 名 論拠，原理，道理
- □ **react** 動 反応する，対処する
- □ **reaction** 名 反応，反動，反抗，影響
- □ **reader** 名 ①読者 ②読本，リーダー

- □ **readily** 副 ①すぐに，さっそく ②快く，進んで **readily visible** 容易に目に見える
- □ **reading** 動 read (読む) の現在分詞 名 読書，読み物，朗読
- □ **ready to** 《be－》すぐに [いつでも] ～できる，～する構えで
- □ **realize** 動 理解する，実現する
- □ **realm** 名 ①領域，範囲 ②王国，領土
- □ **rear** 名 後ろ，背後
- □ **reason for** ～の理由
- □ **reasoning** 名 論法
- □ **recent** 形 近ごろの，近代の
- □ **recommend** 動 ①推薦する ②勧告する，忠告する
- □ **record** 動 記録 [登録] する
- □ **recoup** 動 取り戻す
- □ **recourse** 名 頼ること，頼りになるもの
- □ **recover** 動 ①取り戻す，ばん回する ②回復する
- □ **rectify** 動 ～を正す
- □ **refer** 動 ①《－ to ～》～に言及する，～と呼ぶ ②～を参照する，～に問い合わせる
- □ **reference** 名 言及，参照，照会 **in reference to** ～に関して
- □ **refrain** 動 差し控える，自制する **refrain from** ～を控える
- □ **refuse** 動 拒絶する，断る
- □ **regard** 名 注意，関心 **in regard to** ～に関しては **in that regard** そのことについて
- □ **regardless** 形 無頓着な，注意しない **regardless of** ～に関わらず
- □ **relaxed** 形 くつろいだ，ゆったりした
- □ **relentlessly** 副 容赦なく
- □ **reliable** 形 信頼できる，確かな
- □ **reload** 動 再装填する

141

□ **rely** 動 (人が…に) 頼る, 当てにする **rely on ～** を当てにする, ～を頼りにする

□ **remain** 動 ①残っている, 残る ②(～の) ままである [いる] **remain calm** 冷静さを保つ **remain wary** 依然として慎重である

□ **remove** 動 ①取り去る, 除去する ②(衣類を) 脱ぐ

□ **renew** 動 新しくする, 更新する, 回復する, 再開する

□ **repeat** 動 繰り返す

□ **repeated** 形 繰り返された, 度重なる

□ **require** 動 ①必要とする, 要する ②命じる, 請求する

□ **resolutely** 副 固く決心して

□ **resource** 名 ①資源, 財産 ②手段, 方策

□ **respect** 名 ①尊敬, 尊重 ②注意, 考慮 **with respect to** ～に関して

□ **respond** 動 答える, 返答 [応答] する

□ **response** 名 応答, 反応, 返答

□ **rest** 名 後 (のこと)

□ **restrict** 動 制限する, 禁止する

□ **restring** 動 ～の弦を張り替える

□ **restrung** 動 restring (～の弦を張り替える) の過去動詞

□ **result** 名 結果, 成り行き, 成績

□ **retreat** 動 後退する, 退く

□ **reveal** 動 明らかにする, 暴露する, もらす

□ **reverse** 形 反対の, 裏側の 動 逆にする, 覆す

□ **rhythm** 名 リズム, 調子

□ **rice field** 田

□ **ride out the crisis** 危機を乗り切る

□ **ridge** 名 尾根, 棟 **nose ridge** 鼻筋 **ridge of** ～の背

□ **ridiculously** 副 ばかばかしいほど

□ **riding** 名 乗馬, 乗車

□ **right-thinking** 形 正しい [まともな] 考えを持った

□ **rigid** 形 ①硬い, 固定した ②融通のきかない

□ **ring finger** 薬指

□ **rise in the world** 出世する

□ **roam** 動 ぶらぶら歩き回る, 放浪する

□ **rocky** 形 ①岩の多い ②ぐらぐら揺れる, ぐらつく **rocky terrain** 岩の多い地形

□ **role** 名 ①(劇などの) 役 ②役割, 任務

□ **room** 熟 **formal room** 座敷

□ **roughness** 名 粗いこと, 粗野, でこぼこ, 雑な部分, 不作法

□ **route** 名 道, 道筋, 進路, 回路

□ **row** 動 (舟を) こぐ

□ **ruin** 名 破滅, 滅亡, 破産, 廃墟

□ **rule** 熟 **cardinal rule** 鉄則

□ **runner** 名 走者, 競争者, 集金人, 運転者

□ **running** 動 run (走る) の現在分詞 形 走っている

□ **rush** 動 突進する, せき立てる **rush into** ～に突入する, ～に駆けつける, ～に駆け込む 名 突進, 突撃, 殺到

□ **rushed** 形 大急ぎで行われた [作られた]

S

□ **safekeeping** 名 保管

□ **sake** 名 (～の) ため, 利益, 目的 **for the sake of** ～のために

□ **same ～ as …** 《the –》…と同じ (ような) ～

Word List

□ **samurai** 名侍

□ **sap** 動〜から樹液をしぼり取る, 弱める, なくす

□ **sash** 名帯

□ **say** 熟 needless to say 言うまでもなく

□ **saying** 動 say（言う）の現在分詞 名ことわざ, 格言, 発言

□ **scabbard** 名（刀などの）鞘

□ **scaffolding** 名足場

□ **school** 名流派 a school of fish 魚の群れ

□ **scratch** 動ひっかく, 傷をつける, はがし取る

□ **screen** 名仕切り, 幕, スクリーン, 画面 sliding screen 障子

□ **seamlessly** 副継ぎ目なく, 途切れなく

□ **search** 名捜査, 探索, 調査 in search of 〜を探し求めて

□ **seat** 熟 seat of honor 上席 take a seat 席にすわる

□ **second** 熟 a split second 瞬時

□ **secret** 形秘密の, 隠れた 名秘密, 神秘 inner secret 奥義

□ **see 〜 as …** 〜を…と考える

□ **seek** 動捜し求める, 求める

□ **seem** 動（〜に）見える,（〜のように）思われる seem to be 〜である ように思われる

□ **seize** 動①ぐっとつかむ, 捕らえる ②襲う

□ **select** 動選択する, 選ぶ

□ **self-discipline** 名自己鍛錬

□ **selflessness** 名無欲, 無私

□ **sense** 名①感覚, 感じ ②《-s》意識, 正気, 本性 ③常識, 分別, センス ④意味 make sense 意味をなす, よくわかる not make sense 意味をなさない 動感じる, 気づく

□ **separate** 動①分ける, 分かれる, 隔てる ②別れる, 別れさせる

□ **serious** 形①まじめな, 真剣な ②重大な, 深刻な,（病気などが）重い

□ **seriously** 副①真剣に, まじめに ②重大に

□ **serve** 動仕える, 奉仕する

□ **set** 熟 be set down on paper 紙に書き留められている set down 〜を下に置く, 〜と見なす set oneself up 身を立てる, 背伸びする set out to 〜に着手する, 〜し始める, 〜しようと試みる set to 〜へ向かう, 〜に着手する set up 設置する

□ **settle** 動①安定する［させる］, 落ち着く, 落ち着かせる ②《- in 〜》〜に移り住む, 定住する

□ **shadow** 名影, 暗がり

□ **shallow** 名《the -s》浅瀬

□ **shame** 名恥, 恥辱

□ **shape** 名①形, 姿, 型 ②状態, 調子

□ **sharp** 形①鋭い, とがった ②刺すような, きつい ③鋭敏な ④急な

□ **sharpen** 動①鋭くする, 鋭くなる, とぐ ②厳しくする ③敏感になる

□ **shave** 動（ひげ・顔を）そる, 削る

□ **shelf** 名棚

□ **shelves** 名 shelf（棚）の複数

□ **shift** 動移す, 変える, 転嫁する shift out of 〜から移動する

□ **Shinmen Musashi no Kami, Fujiwara no Genshin** 新免武蔵守藤原玄信（しんめんむさしのかみふじわらのはるのぶ）《宮本武蔵が著書『五輪書』の中で名乗っていた名前。玄信は「はるのぶ」と呼ぶのが正しいが英語版『The Book of Five Rings』では Genshin と訳されている》

□ **Shintō** 名神道

□ **Shintō school** 新当流

□ **Shōhō** 正保《日本の元号の一つ。1644年から1648年まで》

□ **shooting** 名射撃

□ **short** 熟 in short 要約すると

□ **short-handed** 形 手の短い

□ **shoulder** 名 肩

□ **shout** before-after shout 先後の声

□ **shove** 動 乱暴に押す, 押し込む, 突く

□ **show** 熟 put on a show 見せつける, 誇示する　show a preference for ～を好む

□ **showy** 形 目立つ, 派手な, これ見よがしな

□ **shrine** 名 廟, 聖堂, 神社

□ **shrink** 動 ①縮む, 縮小する ②尻込みする, ひるむ　shrink back 身体を縮める

□ **shutter** 名 シャッター, 雨戸, (カメラの) シャッター

□ **side** 名 側, 横, そば, 斜面

□ **sight** 熟 lose sight of ～を見失う

□ **significance** 名 重要(性), 意味, 深刻さ

□ **similar** 形 同じような, 類似した, 相似の　be similar to ～に似ている

□ **simply** 副 ①簡単に ②単に, ただ ③まったく, 完全に

□ **single** 形 たった1つの

□ **single-handedly** 副 独力で, 単独で, 自力で

□ **single-timing attack** 一拍子 (ひとつびょうし) 打ち

□ **singly** 副 一つ一つ, 一人ずつ, 個々に

□ **situation** 名 ①場所, 位置 ②状況, 境遇, 立場

□ **skill** 名 ①技能, 技術 ②上手, 熟練　hone one's skills 自分の技(能)を磨く　polish one's skills 腕を磨く

□ **skillful** 形 熟練した, 腕のいい

□ **slack** 形 ゆるんだ, だらけた, のろい

□ **slap** 動 (平手, 平たいもので) ぴしゃりと打つ

□ **slash** 動 ～をかき切る

□ **sleepiness** 名 眠気, 睡魔

□ **sliding** 滑る, スライドする　sliding door 引き戸, 襖　sliding screen 障子

□ **slight** 形 ①わずかな ②ほっそりして ③とるに足らない

□ **slightly** 副 わずかに, いささか

□ **sling** 動 投げ付ける, つるす

□ **slowly** 副 遅く, ゆっくり

□ **slowness** 名 遅いこと, 緩慢

□ **slung** 動 sling(吊り下げる)の過去・過去分詞

□ **smash** 動 ①粉砕する, 強打する ②撃破する

□ **smithereens** 名 (破壊・爆発などによってできた) 小さな破片　to smithereens 木っ端みじんに

□ **smooth** 動 滑らかにする, 平らにする

□ **smoothly** 副 滑らかに, 流ちょうに

□ **so** 熟 and so そこで, それだから, それで　and so on ～など, その他もろもろ　so that ～するために, それで, ～できるように　so to speak いわば　so ～ that … 非常に～なので…

□ **so-called** 形 いわゆる

□ **social** 形 ①社会の, 社会的な ②社交的な, 愛想のよい

□ **social standing** 社会的地位, 家格

□ **soil** 名 土, 土地

□ **soldier** 名 兵士, 兵卒　foot soldier 足軽

□ **solely** 副 1人で, 単独で, 単に

□ **solid** 形 ①固体 [固形] の ②頑丈な

□ **someone** 代 ある人, 誰か

□ **something** 代 ①ある物, 何か ②いくぶん, 多少

□ **sometimes** 副 時々, 時たま

Word List

□ **somewhat** 副 いくらか, やや, 多少

□ **soon** 熟 as soon as ～するとすぐ, ～するや否や

□ **sort** 名 種類, 品質 a sort of ～のようなもの, 一種の～

□ **space** 熟 confined space 限定空間

□ **spare** 形 暇の, 予備の

□ **speak** 熟 so to speak いわば speak of ～を口にする

□ **spear** 槍で突く, 槍のように突き進む

□ **spearman** 名 槍使い

□ **spearmen** 名 spearman (槍使い)の複数

□ **spectacular** 形 見世物の, 壮観な

□ **speed** 名 速力, 速度 blinding speed 目にも止まらぬ速さ

□ **speedy** 形 速い, 迅速な

□ **spin** 動 ぐるぐる回る, スピンする

□ **spirit** 名 ①霊 ②精神, 気力

□ **split** 形 割れた, 分割した a split second 瞬時

□ **spot** 名 地点, 場所 on the spot その場で, ただちに

□ **square** 形 正方形の, 四角な, 直角な, 角ばった

□ **squeeze** 動 絞る, 強く握る, 締めつける

□ **stab** 名 刺し傷, 突き傷

□ **stage** 名 段階

□ **stagnate** 動 停滞する

□ **stamp** 動 踏みつける

□ **stance** 名 構え take a stance 姿勢をとる

□ **standard** 名 標準, 規格, 規準

□ **standing** 名 地位, 身分 social standing 社会的地位, 家格

□ **state** 名 あり様, 状態

□ **static** 形 静的な, 変化のない static position 静止位置

□ **statue** 名 像

□ **stature** 名 背丈, 身長

□ **steep** 形 険しい, 法外な steep incline 急勾配

□ **steer** 動 舵をとる, 操縦する

□ **stick** 動 ①(突き)刺さる, 刺す ②くっつく, くっつける ③突き出る

□ **stickiness** 名 粘性

□ **sticky** 形 ①くっつく, 粘着性の ②暑苦しい ③やっかいな

□ **stifle** 動 ①窒息させる, 息の根を止める ②鎮圧する

□ **straight** 熟 from straight above 真上から

□ **strait** 名 海峡

□ **strategic** 形 戦略的な, 戦略上の

□ **strategically** 副 戦略的に

□ **strategist** 名 戦略家

□ **strategy** 名 戦略, 作戦, 方針 art of strategy 戦略の技術, 兵法 military strategy 軍事戦略

□ **stray** 動 ①はぐれる, 道に迷う ②さまよう ③わきにそれる, 本筋からはずれる

□ **stream** 名 小川, 流れ

□ **strength** 名 ①力, 体力 ②長所, 強み ③強度, 濃度

□ **strengthen** 動 強くする, しっかりさせる

□ **stretch** 動 引き伸ばす, 広がる, 広げる stretch out ①手足を伸ばす, 背伸びする ②広がる

□ **stride** 名 ①大またで歩くこと ②一またぎ

□ **strike** 動 ①打つ, ぶつかる ②(災害などが)急に襲う chance to strike ～に行き当たる strike up 跳ね上げる 名 打つこと, 打撃

□ **strive** 動 努める, 奮闘する strive for ～を得ようと努力する

□ **strongly** 副 強く, 頑丈に, 猛烈に,

145

S

熱心に

- [ ] **struggle** 名 もがき, 奮闘 **life or death struggle** 死ぬか生きるかの戦い

- [ ] **stuck** 形 行き詰まった, 立ち往生した **be stuck together** くっつき合っている

- [ ] **sturdy** 形 屈強な, 頑丈な

- [ ] **style** 名 やり方, 流儀, 様式, スタイル

- [ ] **subordinate** 名 部下

- [ ] **substance** 名 ①物質, 物 ②実質, 中身, 内容

- [ ] **subtle** 形 微妙な, かすかな, 繊細な, 敏感な, 器用な

- [ ] **success** 名 成功, 幸運, 上首尾

- [ ] **successfully** 副 首尾よく, うまく

- [ ] **such a** そのような

- [ ] **such as** たとえば~, ~のような **such ~ as** ……のような~

- [ ] **such ~ that …** 非常に~なので…

- [ ] **suchlike** 代 そのような種類のもの **and suchlike** ~などなど

- [ ] **sudden** 形 突然の, 急な

- [ ] **suffer** 動 ①(苦痛・損害などを)受ける, こうむる ②(病気に)なる, 苦しむ, 悩む **suffer in** ~で苦しむ

- [ ] **sufficient** 形 十分な, 足りる

- [ ] **suit** 動 適合する [させる]

- [ ] **suitable** 形 適当な, 似合う, ふさわしい

- [ ] **suited** 形 適した

- [ ] **superficial** 形 表面の, うわべだけの

- [ ] **superficially** 副 表面的に

- [ ] **superior** 形 優れた, 優秀な, 上方の

- [ ] **suppress** 動 ①抑える, 抑圧する ②隠す ③我慢する

- [ ] **sure to do** 熟 《be ~》必ず~する

- [ ] **surely** 副 確かに, きっと

- [ ] **surface** 名 ①表面, 水面 ②うわべ, 外見 **on the surface** 外面は, うわべは

- [ ] **swamp** 名 沼地, (低)湿地

- [ ] **swiftly** 副 速く, 迅速に

- [ ] **swing** 動 ①揺り動かす, 揺れる ②回転する, ぐるっと回す 名 揺れ, 振ること, 振動

- [ ] **switch** 動 切り替える, 切り替わる

- [ ] **swoop** 名 急襲 **in one fell swoop** 一挙に

- [ ] **sword** 名 ①剣, 刀 ②武力 **flat of the sword** 刀のひら

- [ ] **swordplay** 名 太刀さばき

- [ ] **swordsman** 名 剣士, 剣術家

- [ ] **swordsmanship** 名 剣の腕前

- [ ] **swung** 動 swing(回転する)の過去, 過去分詞

T

- [ ] **ta-dum ta-dum** とたんとたん 《擬態語》

- [ ] **tabernacle** 名 厨子《仏具》

- [ ] **tachi** 名 太刀

- [ ] **tack** 動 上手回しにする (ジグザグに進ませる)

- [ ] **tacking** 名 「まぎれる」ということ 《つづら折りのように曲がりくねってかかっていく戦い方》

- [ ] **tactic** 名 戦術, 戦法

- [ ] **tactical** 形 戦術上の

- [ ] **tactics** 名 戦術, 戦法

- [ ] **tail wind** 追い風

- [ ] **Tajima** 名 但馬の国《地名。現在の兵庫県北部》

- [ ] **Takasago** 名 高砂《能の作品の一つ》

- [ ] **take** 熟 **It may take ~ days to …**

…するには～日かかるだろう **take a big picture** 全体像を捉える **take a seat** 席にすわる **take a stance** 姿勢をとる **take advantage of** ～を利用する，～につけ込む **take care** 気をつける，注意する **take care to** よく（注意して）［入念に］～する **take in** 取り入れる，取り込む，(作物・金など)を集める **take into consideration** ～を考慮に入れる **take place** 行われる，起こる **take the attitude** その態度を取る **take the initiative** 先手を打つ **take the initiative in** ～においてイニシアチブ［主導権］を取る **take up** 取り上げる，拾い上げる，やり始める，(時間・場所を)とる **take ～ into consideration** ～を考慮に入れる

☐ **taken up with** 《be ～》～に引き付けられる

☐ **talent** 图 才能，才能ある人

☐ **tangible** 形 実体のある，現実の **tangible form** 有形の形式

☐ **task** 图 (やるべき)仕事，職務，課題

☐ **tea ceremony** 茶道

☐ **teaching** 图①教えること，教授，授業 ②《-s》教え，教訓

☐ **technique** 图 テクニック，技術，手法

☐ **temper** 動 ～の厳しさを和らげる，～を調節する

☐ **temple** 图 寺

☐ **tenaciously** 副 執拗に

☐ **tense** 形 緊張した，切迫した，ぴんと張った **tense up** 緊張させる

☐ **tenseness** 图 緊張(性)

☐ **Terao Magonojō** 寺尾孫之丞《諱は勝信(延)，号は夢世。熊本における宮本武蔵の一番の高弟であった。『五輪書』を伝授される》

☐ **Terao Yumeyo Katsunobu** 寺尾夢世勝延《寺尾孫之丞のこと。「夢世」は孫之丞の号》

☐ **term** 图①期間，期限 ②語，用語 ③《-s》条件 ④《-s》関係，仲 **in**

terms of ～の言葉で言えば，～の点から **on equal terms with** ～と同じ条件で，～と対等で

☐ **terrain** 图 地形，地勢 **rocky terrain** 岩の多い地形

☐ **terribly** 副 ひどく

☐ **territory** 图①領土 ②(広い)地域，範囲，領域

☐ **test-fire** 動 試射する

☐ **than** 熟 **no more than** ただの～にすぎない **rather than** ～よりむしろ

☐ **that** 熟 **at that moment** その時に，その瞬間に **in that context** その意味で **in that regard** そのことについて **so that** ～するために，それで，～てきるように **so ～ that** …非常に～なので… **such ～ that** …非常に～なので… **those that** それらの物

☐ **then** 熟 **even then** その時でさえ **now and then** ときどき

☐ **there** 熟 **here and there** あちこちで **there is no way** ～する見込みはない

☐ **thereafter** 副 それ以来，従って

☐ **thereby** 副 それによって，それに関して

☐ **therefore** 副 したがって，それゆえ，その結果

☐ **these days** このごろ

☐ **think of** ～のことを考える，～を思いつく，考え出す

☐ **thinking** 動 think (思う)の現在分詞 图 考えること，思考 形 思考力のある，考える

☐ **this** 熟 **at this point** 現在のところ **in this way** このようにして **like this** このような，こんなふうに

☐ **thorough** 形①徹底的な，完全な ②まったくの

☐ **thoroughly** 副 すっかり，徹底的に

☐ **those that** それらの物

☐ **those who** ～する人々

□ **those with** 〜を持つ人々

□ **though** 接 ①〜にもかかわらず，〜だが ②たとえ〜でも **as though** あたかも〜のように，まるで〜みたいに **even though** 〜であるけれども，〜にもかかわらず

□ **thought** 熟 put one's thoughts on paper 自分の考えを紙に書き留める

□ **thread** 名 糸，糸のように細いもの

□ **threaten** 動 脅かす，おびやかす，脅迫する

□ **threatening** 動 threaten（脅かす）の現在分詞 形 ①脅迫的な ②（天候などが）今にもくずれそうな **life threatening** 生命を危うくする

□ **threshold** 名 ①敷居 ②出発点 ②閾（値）④境界

□ **through** 熟 go through 通り抜ける，一つずつ順番に検討する

□ **throw 〜 off balance** 〜の平衡［均衡］を失わせる

□ **thrust** 動 ①強く押す，押しつける，突き刺す ②張り出す，突き出る **thrust forward** 前に突き出す **thrust out** 〜を突き出す 名 ぐいと押すこと，突き刺すこと

□ **thumb** 名 親指 **the thumb and the index figure** 親指と人差し指《figureはここでは指の一部を表わす》

□ **thus** 副 ①このように ②これだけ ③かくて，だから

□ **tight** 形 堅い，きつい，ぴんと張った

□ **timber** 名 ①材木，木材 ②横木，棟木

□ **time** 熟 at a time 一度に，続けざまに **at times** 時には **at one time or another**（正確な日付は覚えていないが）いつだったか **at the time of** 〜の時［際］に **every time** 〜するときはいつも **for the first time** 初めて **have no time to do** 〜する時間がない **in time** 間に合って，やがて **perfectly timed** 完璧にタイミン

グが合っている

□ **timid** 形 気の小さい，臆病な，おどおどした

□ **timing** 名 タイミング **timing is off** タイミングがずれている

□ **tip** 名 先端，頂点

□ **tireless** 形 疲れを知らない，精力的な，根気強い，絶え間ない

□ **tirelessly** 副 疲れないで，たゆみなく

□ **toe** 名 足指，つま先

□ **together** 熟 be stuck together くっつき合っている

□ **too much** 過度の

□ **tool** 名 道具，用具，工具

□ **toolbox** 名 道具箱

□ **torso** 名 (人の) 胴

□ **totally** 副 全体的に，すっかり

□ **tout** 動 しつこく売り込む

□ **trade** 名 取引，貿易，商業

□ **training** 動 train（訓練する）の現在分詞 名 ①トレーニング，訓練 ②コンディション，体調

□ **trample** 動 踏みつける

□ **trampling** 名 踏みつけること

□ **transform** 動 ①変形［変化］する，変える ②変換する

□ **transmission** 名 ①送信，伝達，通信 ②伝染 **oral transmission** 口伝

□ **transmit** 動 ①送る ②伝える，伝わる ③感染させる **be transmitted orally** 口伝される

□ **traverse** 動 ①横断する，横切る ②前後［左右］に動く

□ **tread** 動 ①歩く，行く ②足を踏み入れる

□ **treat** 動 扱う

□ **trick** 名 ①策略 ②いたずら，冗談

□ **trivial** 形 ①ささいな ②平凡な

□ **triviality** 名 つまらない［ささいな］

Word List

こと
- [ ] **troop** 名 隊
- [ ] **true Way** 《the –》本来の道
- [ ] **truth** 名 ①真理, 事実, 本当 ②誠実, 忠実さ
- [ ] **tuck** 熟 nip and tuck 五分五分で
- [ ] **tune** 名 ①曲, 節 ②正しい調子［旋律］keep in tune with ～と調子を合わせる
- [ ] **turn down** 伏せる
- [ ] **turn one's back on** ～に背を向ける, ～を無視する
- [ ] **turn ～ over in one's mind** ～をよくよく考える
- [ ] **turn up** 上を向く
- [ ] **twist** 動 ねじる, よれる
- [ ] **twisted** 形 ねじれた
- [ ] **two-handed** 形 両手で扱う, 両手使いの

U

- [ ] **unable** 形 《be – to ～》～することができない
- [ ] **unaffected** 形 影響を受けない
- [ ] **unavoidable** 形 避けられない
- [ ] **uncertain** 形 不確かな, 確信がない
- [ ] **uncertainty** 名 不確かさ, 不安
- [ ] **uncomfortable** 形 心地よくない
- [ ] **unconcerned** 形 無関心な, 心配しない be unconcerned about ～に無関心である
- [ ] **uncover** 動 ふたを取る, 覆いを取る
- [ ] **uncuttable** 形 斬られない
- [ ] **underarm** 名 脇の下
- [ ] **underdo** 動 十分に行わない
- [ ] **underfoot** 副 足元に crush ～

underfoot ～を踏みにじる
- [ ] **understanding** 名 理解, 意見の一致, 了解
- [ ] **undertake** 動 ①引き受ける ②始める, 企てる
- [ ] **undertaken** 動 undertake（引き受ける）の過去分詞 be undertaken to ～するために企てられる
- [ ] **undone** 形 ①解かれた, ほどけた ②未完成の leave nothing undone やり残しを残さない
- [ ] **undoubtedly** 副 疑う余地なく
- [ ] **unexpected** 形 思いがけない, 予期しない
- [ ] **unintentionally** 副 故意ではなく, 気付かずに
- [ ] **unless** 接 もし～でなければ, ～しなければ
- [ ] **unmovable** 形 動かされない
- [ ] **unobstructed** 形 邪魔のない
- [ ] **unprotrude** 動 突き出さない
- [ ] **unprotruding** 形 突き出ていない
- [ ] **unrelated** 形 関係のない, 親類でない unrelated to ～と無関係の
- [ ] **unsure** 形 確かでない, 自信がない
- [ ] **until hell freezes over** 永遠に
- [ ] **untrained** 形 訓練されていない, 未熟な
- [ ] **unusual** 形 普通でない, 珍しい, 見［聞き］慣れない
- [ ] **unwavering** 形 揺るぎない
- [ ] **up** 熟 be taken up with ～に引き付けられる come up against ～に直面する,（障害・困難・問題・反対など）に出くわす divide up 分ける end up 結局～になる follow up on ～を実行に移す give up あきらめる, やめる, 引き渡す keep up with ～に遅れずについていく, ～と歩調を合わせる pick up 拾い上げる, 習得する, 再開する, 回復する push up 押

A
B
C
D
E
F
G
H
I
J
K
L
M
N
O
P
Q
R
S
T
U
V
W
X
Y
Z

し上げる **set oneself up** 身を立てる, 背伸びする **set up** 設置する **strike up** 跳ね上げる **take up** 取り上げる, 拾い上げる, やり始める, (時間・場所を)とる **tense up** 緊張させる **turn up** 上を向く

□ **up-thrust** 名突き上げ

□ **uplift** 動持ち上げる, 上昇させる

□ **uplifted** 形持ち上げられた

□ **upon** 前①《場所・接触》〜(の上)に②《日・時》〜に③《関係・従事》〜に関して, 〜について, 〜して **fall upon** 〜に向かって行く, 〜の上にかかる **look down upon** 見下ろす, 俯瞰する 副前へ, 続けて

□ **upper** 形上の, 上位の, 北方の **have the upper hand** 有利[優勢]である

□ **upward** 副上の方へ, 上向きに

□ **urgency** 名①緊急性②しつこさ

□ **urgent** 形緊急の, 差し迫った

□ **usage** 名①使用法②(言語の)慣用, 語法

□ **use** 熟 **make use of** 〜を利用する, 〜を生かす

□ **used** 熟 **get used to** 〜になじむ, 〜に慣れる **used to** ①以前は〜だった, 以前はよく〜したものだった②《be 〜》〜に慣れる

□ **usefulness** 名役に立つこと, 有用性

□ **useless** 形役に立たない, 無益な

□ **user** 名使用者, 利用者, 消費者

□ **utilize** 動利用する, 活用する

□ **utterly** 副まったく, 完全に

V

□ **variability** 名変動性, 可変(性)

□ **variety** 名①変化, 多様性, 寄せ集め②種類

□ **various** 形変化に富んだ, さまざまの, たくさんの

□ **vary** 動変わる, 変える, 変更する, 異なる

□ **veranda** 名ベランダ

□ **verge** 名①へり, 縁, 端②境界③瀬戸際 **on the verge of** 今にも〜しようとして

□ **victor** 名勝者, 優勝者

□ **victorious** 形勝利を得た, 勝った

□ **victory** 名勝利, 優勝 **claim victory** 勝利を収める

□ **view** 熟 **point of view** 考え方, 視点

□ **viewpoint** 名見地, 観点, 見解

□ **violent** 形暴力的な, 激しい

□ **virtue** 名①徳, 高潔②美点, 長所③効力, 効き目

□ **visible** 形目に見える, 明らかな **readily visible** 容易に目に見える

□ **vital** 形①活気のある, 生き生きとした②きわめて重要な

□ **vitally** 副極めて重大で, 絶対に

W

□ **waist** 名ウエスト, 腰のくびれ

□ **wait for** 〜を待つ

□ **waiting** 動wait (待つ)の現在分詞 形待っている, 仕えている

□ **wakizashi** 名脇差し

□ **walking** 動walk (歩く)の現在分詞 名歩行, 歩くこと

□ **wander** 動①さまよう, 放浪する, 横道へそれる②放心する

□ **wanting** 形欠けている

□ **war chronicle** 軍記, 戦記

□ **ward** 動避ける, よける **ward off** 回避する, 防ぐ, かわす

□ **warn** 動警告する, 用心させる

□ **warped** 形そった

Word List

□ **warrior** 名戦士, 軍人

□ **wary** 形用心深い, 慎重な **remain wary** 依然として慎重である

□ **wave** 名波

□ **way** 熟 **in a way** ある意味では **in any way** 決して, 多少なりとも **in this way** このようにして **make one's way** 前進する **the true Way** 本来の道 **there is no way** ～する見込みはない **way of life** 生き様, 生き方, 暮らし方 **way of the world** 慣例, 世の習わし **way to** ～する方法

□ **weaken** 動弱くなる, 弱める

□ **weakly** 副弱々しく

□ **weakness** 名①弱さ, もろさ ②欠点, 弱点

□ **weapon** 名武器, 兵器

□ **wedge** 名くさび, くさび状のもの **close the wedge** くさびをしめる

□ **well** 熟 **as well** なお, その上, 同様に **as well as** ～と同様に **be well -ed** よく[十分に]～された **be well acquainted with** ～によく通じている **not do well** 苦手である

□ **well-known** 形よく知られた, 有名な

□ **what** 熟 **no matter what** たとえ何があろうと **what … for** どんな目的で

□ **whatever** 代①《関係代名詞》～するものは何でも ②どんなこと[もの]が～とも 形①どんな～でも ②《否定文・疑問文で》少しの～も, 何らかの

□ **When it comes to** ～に関して言えば

□ **whenever** 接①～するときはいつでも, ～するたびに ②いつ～しても

□ **where to** どこで～すべきか

□ **whereas** 接～であるのに対して[反して], ～である一方

□ **wherever** 接どこでも, どこへ[で]～するとも 副いったいどこへ

[に・で]

□ **whether** 接～かどうか, ～かまたは…, ～であろうとなかろうと

□ **which** 熟 **in all of which** それら全ての中で **of which** ～の中で

□ **whichever** 代いったいどれが, どちら(どれ)でも, どちらが～しようとも

□ **who** 熟 **those who** ～する人々

□ **whole** 形全体の, すべての, 完全な. 満～, 丸～

□ **wholeheartedly** 副心から

□ **wide** 形幅の広い, 広範囲の, 幅が～ある

□ **wide-open** 形大きく開いた, 開け放された

□ **widely** 副広く, 広範囲にわたって

□ **wield** 動①(道具などを)巧みに使う ②(権力などを)振るう

□ **wielder** 名(武器などをやすやすと)操る[振り回す]人

□ **wildly** 副荒々しく, 乱暴に, むやみに

□ **wildness** 名荒々しさ

□ **will** 名意志

□ **wind** 熟 **a tail wind** 追風

□ **winning** 名勝つこと, 勝利, 《-s》賞金 形勝った, 優勝の

□ **wisdom** 名知恵, 賢明(さ)

□ **wish** 熟 **as you wish** 望み通りに

□ **with** 熟 **be compared with** ～と比較して, ～に比べれば **be familiar with** ～をよく知っている, ～と親しい **be filled with** ～でいっぱいになる **be incompatible with** ～と相いれない **be obsessed with** ～で頭がいっぱいである **be taken up with** ～に引き付けられる **be well acquainted with** ～によく通じている **burst out with** (感情を)急に表す, 激発する **collide with** ～にぶつかる **come in contact with** ～と接触する[触れ合う], ～に出くわ

す **fight with** ～と戦う **hit it off with**（人）と折り合う，～とうまくやる **in a fight with** ～と戦っている **in accordance with** ～に従って **in harmony with** ～と調和して **keep in tune with** ～と調子を合わせる **keep up with** ～に遅れずについていく，～と歩調を合わせる **loaded down with** ～で手一杯である **on equal terms with** ～と同じ条件で，～と対等で **those with** ～を持つ人々 **with respect to** ～に関して

□ **within** 前 ①～の中[内]に，～の内部に ②～以内で，～を越えないで

□ **without** 熟 not … without ～ing ～せずには…しない，～すれば必ず…する **without hesitation** ちゅうちょなく

□ **word** 熟 in other words すなわち，言い換えれば **word of mouth** 口頭

□ **work** 熟 work of ～の作業 **work on** ～で働く，～に取り組む，～を説得する，～に効く

□ **world** 熟 come down in the world 落ちぶれる **in the world** 世界で **in the world at large** 世界中に広く **in the world of business** 商売の世界では **rise in the world** 出世する **way of the world** 慣例，世の習わし

□ **worse** 形 いっそう悪い，より劣った，よりひどい

□ **worship** 動 崇拝する，礼拝[参拝]する，拝む

□ **worth** 形（～の）価値がある，(～)しがいがある

□ **would like** ～がほしい **would like to** ～したいと思う

□ **wrinkle** 名 しわ

□ **wrist** 名 手首，リスト

□ **write down** 書き留める

□ **writing** 動 write（書く）の現在分詞 名 ①書くこと，作文，著述 ②筆跡 ③書き物，書かれたもの，文書 **in writing** 書面で **put down in** writing 書き物にする，書き留める

□ **wrong** 熟 go wrong 失敗する，道を踏みはずす，調子が悪くなる

Y

□ **Yamamoto Gensuke** 山本源介《寺尾孫之丞の門人》

□ **yawn** 名 あくび

□ **yet** 熟 and yet それなのに，それにもかかわらず

□ **ying-yang** 形 陰陽の

□ **youth** 名 若さ，元気，若者

Z

□ **zigzag** 形 ジグザグの 動 ジグザグに進む

English Conversational Ability Test
国際英語会話能力検定

● E-CATとは…
英語が話せるようになるための
テストです。インターネット
ベースで、30分であなたの発
話力をチェックします。

www.ecatexam.com

● iTEP®とは…
世界各国の企業、政府機関、アメリカの大学
300校以上が、英語能力判定テストとして採用。
オンラインによる90分のテストで文法、リー
ディング、リスニング、ライティング、スピー
キングの5技能をスコア化。iTEP®は、留学、就
職、海外赴任などに必要な、世界に通用する英
語力を総合的に評価する画期的なテストです。

www.itepexamjapan.com

ラダーシリーズ

The Book of Five Rings 五輪書

2023年9月7日　第1刷発行

原著者　宮本武蔵

発行者　浦　晋亮

発行所　**IBCパブリッシング株式会社**
〒162-0804 東京都新宿区中里町29番3号
菱秀神楽坂ビル
Tel. 03-3513-4511　Fax. 03-3513-4512
www.ibcpub.co.jp

印刷　株式会社シナノパブリッシングプレス

装丁　伊藤 理恵

Printed in Japan
ISBN978-4-7946-0780-5